D1564000

WHAT TO DO UNTIL JESUS COMES BACK

W. A. Criswell

WHAT TO DO UNTIL JESUS COMES BACK

BROADMAN PRESS
Nashville, Tennessee

© Copyright 1975 ● Broadman Press
All rights reserved
4255-55
ISBN: 0-8054-5555-8

Dewey Decimal Classification: 248.4
Subject Headings: Christian Life/Jesus Christ, Second Coming
Library of Congress Catalog Card Number: 75-8327
Printed in the United States of America

Dedication

"To the editors of our Broadman Press who are willing to allow expression and publication of varying interpretations of Holy Scripture"

—W. A. CRISWELL

Preface

There is a famous work of music written by a Viennese composer named Franz Schubert. It is entitled the "Unfinished Symphony." The naming of that piece of music poignantly reminds me of this present book. The 152 pages of its publication presents but so small a part of an infinitely interesting subject.

While I was gathering the material and assembling the chapters, I suddenly and disappointingly discovered that I had the material for two or three volumes beside. There was no alternative but to stop the preparation and to limit the chapters to the few that are here included. It is my hope that the words written on the pages will stand for a multitude of other ideas and substantiating appeals which are omitted for lack of space.

As with a previously published volume by the Broadman Press entitled, *Why I Preach That the Bible Is Literally True*, let me be careful to avow that the theological position which forms the background and basis of this present book is by no means shared by all Southern Baptists, or even all evangelicals. I am a literalist and not a liberal. I am an exegete, not an eisegete. I am a premillennialist and not a postmillennialist. I believe that if God breaks his promises to Israel, I have no assurance but that he may break his promises to me. I believe there is a literal Jesus who is coming. I believe there is a literal Kingdom to be established. I believe there is a literal, physical resurrection (not just a spiritual resurrection) from the dead and that the church is never broken or separated by death. Some of us are members of the body of Christ here in this earth, some of us are members of the body of Christ there in heaven, but some day when Jesus comes again we shall all be one in the Lord, in the faith, and in his glorious Kingdom.

There are many academicians, theologians, and preachers who do not share this persuasion. As they publish their books and present their views, may God bless them in the wisdom the Holy Spirit has bestowed upon them My point in speaking of my position is simply this: we all have a right to interpret the Scriptures as God gives us ableness to understand them. This present book is based upon the way that I understand the holy and inspired Word of God. This is the way that I preach it Sunday by Sunday and year after year.

It is my prayer, humbly and earnestly laid before the throne of grace, that God will bless the message presented in these pages as gloriously and dramatically as he has blessed the message expounded from the pulpit of the First Baptist Church here in Dallas. Thank you for reading the words and thank you for weighing what is said with an open heart and mind. God bless you all forever and ever.

W. A. CRISWELL

Contents

PART I

THE GLORIOUS PROMISE, AND THE BLESSED HOPE

[WATCH]

"And then shall they see the Son of man coming in the clouds with great power and glory."

Matthew 13:26

"This same Jesus, which is taken up from you into heaven, shall so come in like manner as ye have seen him go into heaven."

Acts 1:11

"Looking for that blessed hope, and the glorious appearing of the great God and our Saviour Jesus Christ . . ."

Titus 2:13

"Behold, the Lord cometh with ten thousands of his saints."

Jude 14

"Behold, he cometh with clouds; and every eye shall see him . . ."

Revelation 1:7

LO! HE COMES

Lo, He comes with clouds descending,
  Once for favored sinners slain;
Thousand thousand saints attending,
  Swell the triumph of His train:
Alleluia! alleluia!
  God appears on earth to reign.

Every eye shall now behold Him,
  Robed in splendor's majesty;
Those who set at naught and sold Him,
  Pierced and nailed Him to the tree,
Deeply wailing, deeply wailing,
  Shall the true Messiah see.

Yea, amen, let all adore Thee,
  High on Thine eternal throne;
Saviour, take the power and glory,
  Claim the kingdom for Thine own:
Oh, come quickly, Oh, come quickly,
  Everlasting God, come down!

CHARLES WESLEY (1707-1788)

1
Is Jesus Really Coming Again?

This same Jesus . . . shall so come in like manner as ye have seen him go . . . (Acts 1:11).

The last that the unbelieving world ever saw of the Lord Jesus was when he was hanging on the cross. They saw him last when he died. It was not the unbelieving world, but it was the disciples who said that on the third day Jesus arose again. It was to the disciples that for forty days, with many infallible proofs, he appeared. It was the disciples who on the fortieth day saw him ascend into heaven when a cloud received him out of their sight. It was these disciples who became changed men with an incomparably glorious testimony. Instead of their returning from the Mount of Olives in grief and in despair, the disciples turned their faces to Jerusalem and to the world with unspeakable joy and gladness. That is such a strange thing, because one would naturally think that they would have mourned the departure of their Lord, that they would have wept and cried because they were separated from him. But not so! They filled Jerusalem with their songs of gladness and rejoicing as the Holy Spirit of God filled their own souls to overflowing.

The secret of their joy and gladness is that they believed that the same Lord Jesus who was separated from them would come again in triumph and in great glory. As they were standing on the Mount of Olives steadfastly gazing up into heaven, into which the Lord had ascended, angels came and said: "Why do you gaze up into glory? This same Lord Jesus shall come again in like manner as you have seen him go." The Lord knows what to speak to his people, and he knows when to speak it. The Lord God revealed to those disciples that this same Jesus, who had just ascended into glory, would come again in like manner, just as they had seen him ascend. The promise of the return of Christ was the central hope and the cardinal doctrine around which those early believers and that primitive church built their indescribably victorious and triumphant enthusiasm.

In the bitter persecution of the church during the first Christian centuries, for a man to trust in Jesus was, for the most part, to forfeit his property and his life. In order to survive at all, Christians had to live secretly in catacombs, in caves, and in hidden places. Therefore, as they traveled in the cities of the Roman empire, they had passwords whereby they were able to recognize one another and to introduce themselves to each other. One of those passwords was this: *achri hou elthei,* "till he come" (cf. 1 Corinthians 11:26). Another one was *Maranatha,* which is made up of two Aramaic words: *marana,* "Lord," and *tha,* "come"; *Maranatha,* "Lord, come!" (cf. 1. Corinthians 16:22). The secret passwords of those disciples who were so bitterly persecuted were these words of the hope and promise of the coming Saviour.

As one Christian would meet another in a dark alley or on a dark street, he would whisper as he passed, *"achri hou elthei,"* "till he come"; *"Maranatha,"* "our Lord comes." Think what it meant to a stranger as he passed through Rome or Ephesus or Caesarea or Alexandria or Philippi to hear that glorious word of promise! To a sojourner it meant kindness, hospitality, and gladness. The golden chain that bound those disciples together in that first primitive church as they faced intolerable and merciless persecution was the comfort and the hope of *Maranatha,* and *achri hou elthei.*

The Blessed Hope in Worship

The church built the assurance that Christ would return into all of its worship. Throughout early liturgical literature one will find presented that precious hope. When they repeated the Lord's Prayer they said, "Thy kingdom come." That is a prayer for the return of the Lord. There can be no kingdom without a king. "Thy kingdom come" is a prayer for the king to come.

Consider next the Apostles' Creed:

> "I believe in God the Father Almight, Maker of heaven and earth; And in Jesus Christ his only (begotten) Son, our Lord; who was conceived by the Holy Ghost, born of the Virgin Mary, suffered under Pontius Pilate, was crucified, dead, and buried; He descended into hell (Hades, spirit-world); the third day He rose again from the dead; He ascended into heaven; and sitteth on the right hand of God the Father Almighty; from thence He shall come to judge the quick and the dead. I believe in the Holy Ghost; the holy (Christian universal) catholic church; the communion of saints; the forgiveness of sins; the resurrection of the body (flesh); and the life everlasting. Amen."

That is called the Apostles' Creed. We hardly ever repeat it in our Baptist churches because we say that we do not use creeds that are man-made. But it would not hurt us to repeat it. There is not a syllable in it but that reflects the truth of God as it is in the Bible. Note especially the part that reads: "He was ascended into heaven; and sitteth at the right hand of God the Father Almighty; from thence He shall come to judge the quick and the dead."

All over Christendom for hundreds and hundreds of years the churches of the Lord have repeated that Apostles' Creed. It is a great avowal of the Christian faith, and right in the middle of it is that blessed hope verbalized, "from thence He shall come to judge."

When I conclude a memorial service in the cemetery I usually just read a Scripture and have a prayer. But for centuries ministers of the gospel have used a Christian committal service, and this is part of it:

"Earth to earth, ashes to ashes, dust to dust; looking for the resurrection in the last day, and the life of the world to come, through our Lord Jesus Christ; at whose second coming in glorious majesty to judge the world, the earth and the sea shall give up their dead; and the mortal bodies of them that sleep in Him shall be changed, and made like unto His own glorious body . . ."

Then, for another instance of the emphasis on the return of the Lord in Christian worship, every time we share in the memorial of the Lord's Supper, by eating the broken bread and by drinking the fruit of the vine, we do show the Lord's death till He come, *till he come* (1 Corinthians 11:26). I am emphasizing all of these things just to remind us that in the heart of the Christian faith and all through its worship there is implanted the expectation of Christ's return.

The Blessed Hope in Scripture

Could it be true that Christ is really to come again? Are we to look for the Lord Jesus literally, actually? Even in the days of the apostles. Simon Peter wrote (2 Peter 3:3-4) that "there shall come in the last day scoffers, walking after their own lusts and saying, where is the promise of his coming? For since the fathers fell asleep (died) all things continue as they were from the beginning of the creation," however many years that may have been. Peter then went on to avow that by God's clock a day is as a thousand years, and a thousand years is as a day. We are not to forget that God has his own time clock, which to us may seem slow, but to God is never delayed. The promise of the Second Advent is certain and will not fall to the ground. It will never fail. By God's clock Jesus has been gone two days.

He may return the third day. But, however the time, we are
to look for his coming.

Canon Liddon (1829-1890), one of the great preachers of his
day, preaching at St. Paul's Cathedral in London said, "If Christ
is not coming again in glory, then let us turn the key in the
west door of this cathedral." I would like to make that apply
to all of our worship and to all of our faith. If the Lord Jesus
is not coming again, let us now have the benediction, may we
go our separate ways, may we forget about the faith, about
the Bible, about Christ, about every hope that we have in him,
because all of our doctrines, and all of our promises, and all
of our hopes are bound up in that ultimate and faithful word
of the Lord Jesus Christ that, "If I go away, I will come again;
I will not leave you comfortless" (cf. John 14:3,18).

Now I have three things to say about the promise of Christ
that he will return. First, the infallability, integrity, and moral
authority of the Son of God are bound up in his keeping that
word that he will come again. If he does not, if there is nothing
to his promise, if the word falls to the ground, we have no cause
to worship him as Lord, nor do we have any reason to be
persuaded that any other thing that he said is true. So much
of what the Lord had to say he so earnestly, fervently, and
prayerfully bound up in words describing the ultimate denoue-
ment of the age, the great consummation of this world.

For example, in Mark 8 when he is pleading with men to
confess him openly, the Lord says, "Whosoever . . . shall be
ashamed of me and of my words in this adulterous and sinful
generation; of him also shall the Son of man be ashamed, when
he comes in the glory of the Father with the holy angels" (verse
38). We are to own him, says the Lord, because some day in
glory and in majesty the Lord would like to own us. But if
we are ashamed of him, he will be ashamed of us!

In Matthew 24, the apocalyptic discourse of Jesus, the Lord
speaks at length of his return. The disciples ask him in verse
3, "When shall these things be, and what shall be the sign of

thy coming and of the end of the world?" When the Lord replies, he describes those terrible days of tribulation that were to fall upon Jerusalem in its destruction, a prophecy which came to pass a few years later.

After describing this, he bound up the fate of Jerusalem as a parable, a harbinger, a picture of that final and ultimate tribulation that will come upon all this earth (verses 14, 21-22). The Lord continues by saying that his coming will be open and public, as the lightning bursts out of the east, across the bosom of the sky, and shines unto the west (verse 27). Then he speaks of the great convulsion of nature's structure. The sun is darkened, the stars fall, and the powers of the heavens are shaken (verse 29). Next he speaks of the unexpectedness and the suddenness of his return. It will be as it was in the days of Noah. They were marrying, giving in marriage, and they were having the "night-clubingest" time one could ever imagine. Then the flood came (verses 36-39). In the days of Lot in Sodom and Gomorrah where the patriarch lived, the people were practicing horrible and ungodly sins. Then the fire fell (cf. Luke 17:28-30). So shall it be at the coming of the Son of Man.

Look at these tremendous parables of the Lord in Matthew 25: the parable of the wise and the foolish virgins, the parable of the talents (in Luke there is a similar parable called the parable of the pounds), and finally the parable of the sheep and the goats. See also the parable in Matthew 13 concerning the tares and the wheat. All of these parables have one great, central purpose and teaching. Some interpreters may read these parables and draw extraneous lessons from them, but we are not to forget that the parables were told with one thunderous message which is always the same. They speak of the suddenness of the judgment of the Lord Jesus Christ when he returns.

When the Lord spoke with his disciples privately, he did not change his message. He tenderly reminded them not to be in sorrow. He comforted them with the promise that he was surely coming again. Even in the last interview that he had with Simon and John (cf. John 21:20-23), speaking of John, Jesus said to Simon, "If I will that he tarry till I come, what is that to thee?" His coming is ever uppermost in the mind and in the heart of the Savior.

In the Bible, there is no such person as a Jesus who was not born of the virgin Mary. There is no such person in the Bible as a Jesus who did not work miracles, or who did not rise from the dead. Just as surely, in the Bible there is no such person as a Jesus who is not coming again in glory and in triumph.

We turn now to a second avowal concerning the promise of Christ that he will come again. If we can find any explanation for the incomparable works, the mighty achievements, and the flaming love of those first disciples, we will find it in their persuasion that Jesus was to return in glory, in triumph, and in great power. Luke begins the story of the Acts of the Apostles by recounting how the Lord came and spoke to them saying, "You are to be my preachers and my witnesses (my *martyrs* the Greek has it), here in Palestine and around the earth." After Jesus said that, he was taken up out of their sight. Then Luke describes the angels who came and said, "Ye men of Galilee, why stand ye gazing up into glory? This same Jesus . . . shall so come in like manner as ye have seen him go into heaven." Luke begins the story of the apostles with that precious and blessed promise, and thereafter in every sermon the disciples preached and in every syllable of every word of every sentence that they left behind, you will find a reflection and an echo of that glorious hope and that heavenly avowal.

Because Jesus is coming again, the Christian believers are encouraged to endure affliction and persecution. Because he is coming again, they are enjoined to live godly, sober, and righteous lives. Because he is coming again, they are reminded that they have not lost forever those whom they have loved. They are not to sorrow as others who have no hope. Because He is coming, the minister of Christ is able to comfort broken hearts. We shall see again, in that glorious day of the return of the

Lord, those whom we have loved and lost for just awhile.

There are 318 passages in the New Testament that either directly or indirectly reflect the promise of the return of the Lord. The Bible does not use any such words as the "second coming" of Christ; it is always *the* coming, *the* appearing, *the* presence of the Lord. That event so overshadowed every other event, it was so far beyond anything else in all of God's program, that it became just "the coming," "the appearing," "the presence" of the Lord.

The Blessed Hope in Life

Now my third avowal concerning the promise of Christ that he will come again is this: if there is to be any ultimate triumph of righteousness in the world, if there is to be any kingdom of God among men, if there is to be any true reign of heaven, *then it depends upon the personal intervention of God and the personal presence of the Lord in human history, even Jesus Christ reigning in power and in glory.* May I speak of that in two ways?

First, I speak regarding sin, iniquity, unrighteousness, and wickedness. It is not true so much anymore, but in the past there were some who did earnestly and prayerfully convince themselves that this world would finally ripen into perfection, that the ape and the tiger would be evolved out of the heart and soul of mankind. Just give us centuries of time, they said, and we would gradually evolve into angelic persons who know not sin and who live in a perfect and holy world.

When you think of that, there are two things to be said about it. The first is this: history and experience deny it. In the history of the technical progress of mankind, there is noticeable advancement from immaturity to maturity. There is technical development to be observed everywhere. Start with a one cylinder "horseless carriage," and watch it gradually develop until finally you have these modern automobiles going down the highways just as fast as the state can build roads to receive their onrush.

We can all see that. Look again. There will be a crate of an airplane made by the Wright Brothers, and it will fly every bit of a hundred yards. Gradually it will develop and develop and develop until finally there is built a super rocket that we may ride from here to "kingdom come" and back in five split seconds! They say it is on the way! One can envisage that.

Nevertheless, any discerning eye can also see something else. There is also progress and development in all of those dark and bitter things of Satan, of sin, of unrighteousness, of greed, and of hatred. There is a development there, just as there is a development anywhere else. The violent, evil man who would tarry in the dark with a big club in his hand, or who would hide with a rock on a cliff to drop it down on the head of his neighbor as he passed by, does not have to use a club or a rock anymore. He can take a little revolver and accomplish the same thing. Or he can take nitroglycerin and blow up a bank vault, or, if he is politically viable, he can take bombs and jet planes and persuade 100,000,000 people to support him—can destroy and burn and pillage beyond anything ever dreamed of in this earth.

There is development, but there is never a change of human nature—never. Whether we look into our distant past or project the future as long as mankind shall inhabit this earth, we will find the same greed and the same selfishness, hatred, and planned destruction! We do not change. We were fallen people yesterday, we are fallen people today. We are lost people forever *unless God intervenes.* There is not a syllable of evidence that we ever progress from our innate human nature that is fallen to become angelic and celestial beings that we think of as being holy in the presence of God. We are still just as much lost sinners now as we were thousands of years ago. We do not change.

The second thing I would emphasize about the necessity of a personal intervention by Christ to destroy the kingdom of darkness is that: *such a doctrine is clearly taught in the Word of God.* Jesus said that when the end comes, there will be the tares and there will be the wheat growing up together side by side. That is at the end time. Jesus proclaimed in Matthew 24 that in that final consummation there will be tribulation and great sorrow among the peoples of this earth. Paul said that at the end time there will be sad apostasy in the church. He further taught that there will be a summation, a personalization of all sin in one he called the Man of Sin, the Antichrist. At the last time there will be scoffers and unbelievers, and the love of many will become cold.

John in the Revelation pictures a great and final conflict. The beast and the false prophet are leaders of world organizations apart from the spirit of Christ. It is by His flaming presence in the day of His coming that Christ destroys the beast and the false prophet, and places Satan in the bottomless pit and chains him there for a thousand years. Then, according to John, after the thousand-year reign of Christ, Satan is loosed from his chains for a short time, but is then cast into the lake of fire (hell) forever and ever. All this is wrought by the personal appearing of the Lord Jesus Christ!

Apart from the personal intervention of Christ, human nature remains evil, vile, and full of murder, misery, and misanthropy. We are still people who are fallen. Scientific advancement may have raised our standards of living. Many of the peoples of the earth may share in the proliferation of mechanical gadgets. Nevertheless there is also a terrible cringing before these scientific Frankenstein's monsters that we are capable of creating with our own evil hands.

The Blessed Hope in Death

We turn now to a final consideration concerning the necessity for the coming of our Lord. This is a consideration at the most personal level of all. Apart from the return of Christ, what are we going to do about death, about age, about tears, and sorrow? If the world evolves and evolves, do you think that finally we will ever evolve out of death? Do you think progress will wipe the tears away from our eyes? And if you do believe progress will finally take death out of the world and that there will just naturally be no more death and no more sorrow, no more tears and no more crying, may I ask you one other question? What about those of us who have died before that great and final perfection ever comes? What about us? For we shall die and shall have never seen it. Such a deliverance could never be in my day; neither could it be in my children's day, nor in your children's day, nor in their children's children's day. This perfection which supposedly takes death out of the world could never come for us. We shall all die if the Lord delays. Our children shall die if the Lord delays. If the perfection and holiness of God is something which is to evolve naturally, then all of us who now live shall die before that great and triumphant hour comes. It means that we shall be left behind. It would mean that God has blotted us out. It would mean that we are dead *and dead forever.* We could have no part in the kingdom. God's purpose and promises would only be for some vastly distant future generation.

Is that the blessed hope? Is that the comfort of the Word? Are we preaching the gospel to people who are going to die and die forever? Is Jesus saving people who will be saved for this lifetime, but in the life that is to come, will be blotted out of God's Book and their names remembered no more? Is that the blessed hope? No sir, not by the Book!

Evidently the church at Thessalonica had sent word to Paul saying: "We believe in the return of the Lord, but these beloved of ours have died, and the Lord has not come yet. What about them?" Paul's reply is found in 1 Thessalonians 4:13-18; "My brethren, I would not have you without this knowledge concerning them that fall asleep. [And unless the Lord comes in our lifetime, we, too, shall be in that number who sleep in Jesus.] Let us sorrow not, even as others who have no hope. For if we believe that Jesus died and rose again, even so them also which sleep in Jesus will God bring with Him. [Paul says they are with the Lord now, and when He comes He will bring them with Him.] This we say unto you by the word of the Lord, [that is, God said it himself], that we who are alive and remain unto the coming of the Lord [the generation that is here when the Lord comes] shall not precede them that sleep in Jesus. For the Lord himself shall descend from heaven with a shout, with the voice of the archangel, and with the trump of God: and the dead in Christ shall rise first."

We are all going to share in that ultimate Kingdom—all of us. There will not be a bone left in the region of death for Satan to gloat over. The devil will never be able to say, "This is a part of one of God's children; here is one of his bones I have in my hand." No sir! We shall all be resurrected, and every part of us quickened. Then, also, we who are alive and remain until the coming of the Lord shall be changed in a moment, in the twinkling of an eye. Those who have fallen asleep in the Lord will be resurrected, immortalized, glorified. We who remain shall be no less gloriously changed. Thereafter we shall all be in the presence of the Lord.

The Kingdom of God is for the quick (the living) and for the dead, for us and for our fathers. It is for us and for our children. We belong to one great unperishing, unfading, living Kingdom in the presence of God. In him we never die, for we are with the Lord. When we look up to heaven and look into the face of God, and when we read this blessed promise that he is coming again, we share with John this answering prayer, "Even so come, Lord Jesus." We are praying for this great and final victory.

As Paul says in 1 Corinthians 15:24, "Then cometh the end," and it is as much a part of our faith to believe that, as it is for us to believe that in the beginning God created this world in which we live. As with the beginning of the ages, so the great, final consummation of the last age is in God's precious and blessed hands. Of that God says so much. Concerning the details of the victory, God may hide so much. Nevertheless, God's purpose and plan will be accomplished according to his sovereign grace. That is God's promise to us, and it will be ours in reality when Christ comes again.

2
Literally, As the Prophets Said, So Did Christ Come

And he said unto them, These are the words which I spake unto you, while I was yet with you, that all things must be fulfilled, which were written in the law of Moses, and in the prophets, and in the psalms, concerning me. Then opened he their understanding, that they might understand the scriptures, And said unto them, Thus it is written, and thus it behoved Christ to suffer, and to rise from the dead the third day: And that repentance and remission of sins should be preached in his name among all nations, beginning at Jerusalem (Luke 24:44-47).

The Bible bases its authenticity and authority on prophecy, and in this it is unlike all other sacred books. If authors of other sacred books attempted to foretell future events, their non-fulfillment would have discredited their writings. We see the importance of the study of prophecy in that two-thirds of the Scriptures are prophetic, either in type, symbol, or direct statement. The religious leaders of Christ's day were not students of prophecy, and that is why they failed to recognize Jesus when he came. And if the religious leaders of our day reject the study of prophecy, they will not be ready for Christ's second coming.

Christ is the center of all history, as well as the central theme of the Bible. The Christ of the New Testament is the fruit of the tree of prophecy. The fact of fulfilled prophecy presents irrefutable proof of divine inspiration of the Scriptures, a proof that is conclusive and overwhelming. The coming of Christ, promised in the Old Testament and fulfilled in the New—his

27

birth, character, works, teachings, suffering, death, and resurrection—are the grand central themes of the Bible. The Old
Testament is in the New revealed, and the New Testament is
in the Old concealed. The men who wrote about Jesus in the
Old Testament lived hundreds of years before those who wrote
about him in the New Testament. Yet they wrote about the
same Person.

It is undeniably true that the most ordinary reader may exam-
ine the predictions of the Messiah's person and work found in
the Old Testament, follow the gradual progress of these revelations from Genesis to Malachi, and trace the prophecies as they
descend into details more and more specific and minute, until
at last the full figure of the Coming One stands out. Then, with
this image clearly fixed in his mind's eye, he may turn to the
New Testament and, beginning with Matthew, see how the
historic person, Jesus of Nazareth, corresponds and coincides
in every particular with the prophetic personage depicted by
the prophets. There was no contact between the prophets of
the Old Testament and the narrators of the New Testament.
The reader has not gone out of the Bible itself. He has simply
compared two portraits; one in the Old Testament of a Coming
One, another in the New Testament of one who has actually
come; and his irresistable conclusion is that these two blend
in absolute unity.

All of the prophecies concerning Christ's first coming have
been literally fulfilled. Let us review just a few of them in order
that we may see how God faithfully keeps his word and promise.

The Portrayal of the Coming Christ in the Old Testament

Genesis 3:15 is the first direct Messianic promise in the Bible.
That verse is "the Bible in embryo," the sum of all history and
prophecy in a sentence. Here we have intimated, not only the
virgin birth of Christ, but also his vicarious sufferings—"thou
shalt bruise His heel;" and his complete, eventual victory over

Satan—"it (Messiah) shall bruise thy head."

After the flood, God tells us in Genesis 9:26-27 that the promised seed of the woman would come through the line of Shem. Later, God chooses Abraham to be the father of the Hebrew nation, from whom the Savior would come (Genesis 12:1-3). God thereafter divides the nations of the world into two groups—Jews and Gentiles. Next, Messiah was to come through Isaac, the son of Abraham (Genesis 17:18-21, 26:1-4). Isaac had two sons, Jacob and Esau, and the Abrahamic covenant passes over Esau, the "first born," and falls on Jacob (Genesis 28:12-14). To Jacob were born twelve sons, and God selects Judah (Genesis 49:8-10, 1 Chronicles 5:2) to be the patriarch through whom the Messianic promise is to be realized.

Now the promise gets more definite. It is amazing that the Messiah is to come through Judah and not through Levi (the priestly tribe). The word "sceptre" (Genesis 49:10) indicates kingly power. The promise now skips to the time of David who was of the tribe of Judah. "Thine house and thy kingdom shall be established forever before thee; thy throne shall be established forever" (2 Samuel 7:16).

This promise God later confirmed with an oath, saying:

"I have made a covenant with my chosen, I have sworn unto David my servant, Thy seed will I establish for ever, and build up thy throne to all generations" (Ps. 89:3-4).

"Once I have sworn by my holiness that I will not lie unto David. His seed shall endure for ever, and his throne as the sun before me. It shall be established for ever as the moon, and as a faithful witness in heaven" (Ps. 89:35-37).

Upon the death of David, his son Solomon ascended to the throne. After Solomon's reign, the kingdom was divided into the northern kingdom and the southern kingdom. In 587 B.C.

the last king of Judah was carried into captivity in Babylon. The Jews have not had a king since (Hosea 3:4). Then Jeremiah prophesies about a future king who will sit on the throne of David: "Behold, the days come, saith the Lord, that I will raise unto David a righteous Branch, and a King shall reign and prosper, and shall execute judgment and justice in the earth. In his days Judah shall be saved, and Israel shall dwell safely: and this is his name whereby he shall be called, THE LORD OUR RIGHTEOUSNESS" (Jeremiah 23:5-6).

Also in Isaiah 11:1-2 we see the same word "Branch."

"And there shall come forth a rod out of the stem of Jesse, and a Branch shall grow out of his roots: And the spirit of the Lord shall rest upon him, the spirit of wisdom and understanding, the spirit of counsel and might, the spirit of knowledge and of the fear of the Lord" (Isaiah 11:1-2).

Now look at the description by Luke of the child Jesus. "And the child grew and waxed strong in spirit, filled with wisdom: and the grace of God was upon him" (Luke 2:40). We have no difficulty in identifying whom the prophet meant.

According to the Old Testament, Christ was to be born of a virgin (Isaiah 7:14). Compare this with Matthew 1:18-23. Since Messiah was to be the fruit of David's body (Psalm 132:11) the virgin must be a direct descendant of King David. Turning to the New Testament, we find that Jesus was born of a virgin who was a direct descendant of King David (Matthew 1). In Matthew 1:16-23 and Luke 1:28-35 we see both the prediction and literal fulfillment. The God who gave the specification in Isaiah 7:14 fulfilled it in the virgin birth of Jesus. We see the truth of Jeremiah 1:12: "Jehovah said . . . I watch over my word . . . to perform it." When Messiah came he fulfilled to the letter all the specifications of his lineage and was indeed "the seed of the woman," the son of Abraham, the son of David

(Matthew 1:1).

Let us illustrate. There are no two people exactly alike in all the world—not even identical twins. Suppose your name is Joe Doe. You live at 5901 Swiss Avenue, Dallas, Texas. You are five feet ten inches tall; you weigh one hundred seventy-five pounds. You are married and have one child and two grandchildren. You sell soul insurance. You have $1,243.39 in the bank and you owe $10,251.48! Manifestly no one else in all the world has all of your exact specifications. It is easy to see, if enough characteristic details are given, identification is positive. The same is true of prophecy. If a sufficient number of details are given, identification is positive. In the prophets many, many details of Messiah are given, and each one is exactly fulfilled in Jesus of Nazareth. Identification, therefore, is sure and certain.

The Fulfillment of the Prophetic Picture of Christ in the New Testament

The place of his birth is given (Micah 5:2). The prophet pinpoints one small village on the map. The fulfillment is in Matthew 2:1-6. Until shortly before the time of Jesus' birth, Mary was living at the wrong place; that is, if her coming baby were the Messiah. But look at the intricacies of God's providence in fulfilling His Word. God put it into the heart of Caesar Augustus to take a census of the world and by the time the accustomed way of taking a census in Israel had come to pass, exactly enough delay was caused. In the natural course of events, when the enrollment was put in force in Judaea, the exact time had come for Mary to give birth to Jesus. God who rules the world behind the scene had his hand on the Roman Empire, and he literally moved the people of the world, timed everything to the very day, so that Mary and Joseph arrived in Bethlehem in order that Jesus might be born in the right place, the place designated by the infallible finger of prophecy. The time of his birth is predicted in Daniel 9:25-26. After Jesus was born, great persons were to visit and adore him (Psalm 72:10, Matthew 2:1-11). Through the rage of a jealous king, innocent children were to be slaughtered (Jeremiah 31:15, Matthew 2:16-18). He was to be preceded by a forerunner, John the Baptist (Isaiah 40:3, Malachi 3:1, Luke 1:17, Matthew 3:1-3). He was to be a prophet like Moses (Deuteronomy 18:18, Acts 3:20-22).

He was to have a special anointing of the Holy Spirit (Psalm 45:7, Isaiah 11:2, Matthew 3:16, Luke 4:15-21). He was to be a priest after the order of Melchizedek (Psalm 110:4, Hebrews 5:5-6). He was to be Redeemer for the Gentiles as well as the Jews (Isaiah 42:1-4, Matthew 12:18-21). His ministry was to begin in Galilee (Isaiah 9:1-2, Matthew 4:12,16-23). Later he was to enter Jerusalem (Zechariah 9:9, Matthew 21:1-5) to bring salvation.

Messiah must come while the second Temple was still standing (Haggai 2:7-9, Malachi 3:1, Matthew 21:12). Haggai 2:7-9 says, "the Lord shall suddenly come to his temple." This prediction could not be fulfilled after the destruction of the Temple in 70 A.D. so he had to come before the Temple was destroyed, and he did.

His ministry was to be characterized by miracles (Isaiah 35:5-6, Matthew 11:4-6, John 11:47). He was to be rejected by his brethren (Psalm 69:8, Isaiah 53, John 1:11, John 7:5) and he was to be "a stone of stumbling" to the Jews and a "rock of offence" (Isaiah 8:14, Romans 9:32, 1 Peter 2:8). He was to be hated without a cause (Psalm 69:4, Isaiah 49:7, John 7:48, John 15:25), rejected by the rulers (Psalm 118:22, Matthew 21:42), betrayed by a friend (Psalm 41:9, Psalm 55:12, 14, John 13:8, 21), forsaken by his disciples (Zechariah 13:7, Matthew 26:31-56), sold for thirty pieces of silver (Zechariah 11:12, Matthew 26:15), smitten on the cheek (Micah 5:1, Matthew 27:30), and mocked by his enemies (Psalm 22:7-8, Matthew 27:31, 39-44).

His death by crucifixion is described in Psalm 22, and the

meaning of his death as a substitutionary atonement is given in Isaiah 53. Fourteen times in Isaiah 53 there is announced the doctrine of the offering of Christ as a vicarious sacrifice for all human sin. Never was this mystery solved until Jesus was "made sin for us" (2 Corinthians 5:21) and "died for our sins" (1 Corinthians 15:3, 1 Peter 2:24). So the cross became Christ's deepest humiliation, yet his highest glory and the appointed means of bringing salvation to men.

What the prophets mostly emphasized was the glories of the Messiah and the kingdom he was to usher in. They expected their Messiah to come in power and glory and make the Jewish nation the greatest nation in the world. But when he came in a lowly fashion, they despised and rejected him and nailed him to a cross. They did not realize that thereby they were fulfilling the Scriptures that spoke of the suffering Savior.

His hands and feet were pierced (Psalm 22:16, John 19:18, John 20:25), but not a bone was broken (Exodus 12:46; Psalm 34:20, John 19:33-36). He was given vinegar to drink (Psalm 69:21, Matthew 27:34). He was numbered with transgressors (Isaiah 53:12, Matthew 27:38). His body was to be buried with the rich (Isaiah 53:9, Matthew 27:57-60), but was not to see corruption (Psalm 16:10, Acts 2:31).

He was to be raised from the dead (Psalm 2:7, Psalm 16:10, Acts 13:33) and to ascend to the right hand of God (Psalm 68:18, Luke 24:5, Psalm 110:1, Hebrews 1:3). Thus the life of our Lord was lived in complete conformity to the will of God according to the prophecies of the Old Testament.

Christ Jesus as Prophet, Priest, and King

In Old Testament times, God provided basic needs of mankind through his chosen prophets, priests, and kings. But all human instruments come short and fail. So God planned from the beginning that he would provide the perfect Prophet, Priest, and King for mankind in the perfect One, his only begotten

Son.

(1) Christ as Prophet—The Old Testament prophet represented God to the nation, and he gave God's words and God's message to the people. When the Messiah came, he would represent God perfectly and completely in Person, as well as in Words, to Israel and to the world. When Jesus came he proved to be God's perfect Prophet (John 1:18, John 14:9-10). As Prophet, the Messiah would be like Moses (Deuteronomy 18:15, 18-19). Read John 1:21. Though Moses was great, Christ was infinitely greater. He was the perfect and omniscient Prophet (Acts 3:22-23). Both Isaiah 61:1 and Luke 4:18 refer to Christ's prophetic ministry.

(2) Christ as Priest—The Old Testament priest, chosen by God, represented the people to God and offered sacrifices for their sins. This priesthood, of which Aaron was the first high priest, was imperfect, for the priests themselves were sinners, and so they had first of all to offer sacrifices for their own sins (Hebrews 5:3, 7:26). Their priesthood was short-lived, and was frequently interrupted by death (Hebrews 7:23). The offerings they offered were merely types, for "it is not possible that the blood of bulls and goats should take away sins" (Hebrews 10:4). But in Christ, God's appointed High Priest, we have not only the perfect High Priest who liveth forever, but the one who gave himself for our sins, the perfect offering, the once-for-all complete atonement for the sins of the race (Hebrews 7:26-28, Hebrews 9:11-14, Hebrews 9:25-26, Hebrews 10:10-14). Messiah gave both his body and his soul as an offering for sin and sinners (Isaiah 53:5, 10).

(3) Christ as King (Psalm 2:6)—God, who first ruled the people of Israel through the patriarchs, and later through leaders like Moses and later through judges, finally consented to give them a king. In God's Messiah we have the perfect king (Jeremiah 23:5-6, Isaiah 11:2-5). The word "Messiah" refers to God's anointed King, (I Samuel 2:10, Psalm 45, 47, and 72) the same meaning as the Greek word "Christ."

According to the words of the prophets, the Savior presented himself in the beginning of the Gospels as being the awaited King, but he was rejected and crucified. The Kingdom is now postponed but will be established when Jesus comes back to earth after the tribulation period.

With no variations or aberrations between the Old Testament predictions of the coming King and the New Testament fulfillment in Jesus of Nazareth, one instinctively leaps to the conclusion that the hand that drew the image in prophecy molded the portrait in history, and the inevitable conclusion is four-fold.

(1) It proves the Bible is the inspired Word of God.

(2) It proves that the God of the Bible, the only one who knows the end from the beginning and who alone has the power to fulfill all his Word, is the true and living God.

(3) It demonstrates that the God of the Bible is both all-knowing—to be able to foretell the future entwined around men who are free, moral agents—and all-powerful to be able to bring to pass a perfect fulfillment of his Word in the midst of widespread unbelief and rebellion on the part of men.

(4) It demonstrates that the Person, Jesus of Nazareth, who so perfectly and completely fulfilled all the Old Testament predictions is indeed the Messiah, the Savior of the world, the Son of the living God.

Literally, really, actually did our Savior come the first time into the world to save us from our sins. But there is more, much more. God is not yet finished in his redemptive work among men. There is a Kingdom and a King yet to come. Let us learn what God would have us know about the heavenly triumph he purposes for the saints in this earth.

3
Literally, As the Scriptures Say, So Will Christ Come Again

And while they looked stedfastly toward heaven as he went up, behold, two men stood by them in white apparel; Which also said, Ye men of Galilee, why stand ye gazing up into heaven? this same Jesus, which is taken up from you into heaven, shall so come in like manner as ye have seen him go into heaven (Acts 1:10-11).

There is no fact in history more clearly established than the fact of the "first coming" of Christ. But as his "first coming" did not fulfill all the prophecies associated with his "coming," it is evident that there must be another "coming" completely to fulfill the Scriptures. The Second Coming necessitated the First, and the First demands the Second. Christ Jesus came into the world as a suffering servant. How is he to be also a reigning King? The fulfilled prophecies of his eternal reign in glory and in power will bring to us the blessed Lord Jesus a second time—apart from sin to establish his everlasting kingdom in righteousness and in peace. All the prophecies concerning his first advent were faithfully and literally fulfilled; just so will all the details of Holy Scripture concerning his second advent be fulfilled.

The Double Promise of the Two-fold Coming of the Messiah

It has always been the purpose of God to send a Savior into the world to deliver us from our sins and to set up a divine kingdom on earth. This two-fold purpose is so often seen in the double prophecies of Holy Scripture which describe both

a coming Savior and a coming King. Genesis 3:15 is the first
direct Messianic promise in the Bible. It is called the "Protevan-
gelium" (the first gospel). It is the first pronouncement of the
virgin birth of Christ. In this verse there are two prophecies,
one concerning the First Coming, the other concerning the
Second Coming. The promise of the First Coming is the bruising
of the heel of the woman's seed, who is Jesus Christ. This promise
was literally fulfilled almost 2,000 years ago when the Lord Jesus
was nailed to the cross of Calvary and his heel bruised. There
is another promise in the verse, one not yet completely fulfilled—the bruising of the serpent's head. This will ultimately
be fulfilled at the Second Coming of Christ (Revelation 20:10).

Just as the first promise in the Old Testament contains the
assurance of his Second Coming, so the last promise in the Old
Testament also speaks of the Lord's Second Coming (Malachi
4:2). He is called the "Sun of Righteousness." Between these
two promises in Genesis 3:15 and Malachi 4:2, there are
hundreds of others. For example, in Isaiah 9:6 we read a prophecy of the First Coming and a prophecy of the Second Coming.
The announcement of Jesus' birth is accompanied by the prophecy of his Second Coming as King to reign over the earth. Isaiah
9:6-7 says:

> "For unto us a child is born, unto us a son is given:
> and the government shall be upon his shoulder: and his
> name shall be called Wonderful, Counsellor, The mighty
> God, The everlasting Father, The Prince of Peace. Of the
> increase of his government and peace there shall be no
> end, upon the throne of David, and upon his kingdom,
> to order it, and to establish it with judgment and with
> justice from henceforth even for ever. The zeal of the Lord
> of hosts will perform this" (Isaiah 9:6-7).

The key that unlocks this passage is Luke 1:26-33:

> "And in the sixth month the angel Gabriel was sent

from God unto a city of Galilee, named Nazareth,

"To a virgin espoused to a man whose name was Joseph, of the house of David; and the virgin's name was Mary.

"And the angel came in unto her, and said, Hail, thou that art highly favoured, the Lord is with thee: blessed art thou among women.

"And when she saw him, she was troubled at his saying, and cast in her mind what manner of salutation this should be.

"And the angel said unto her, Fear not, Mary: for thou hast found favour with God.

"And, behold thou shalt conceive in thy womb, and bring forth a son, and shalt call his name JESUS.

"He shall be great, and shall be called the Son of the Highest: and the Lord God shall give unto him the throne of his father David:

"And he shall reign over the house of Jacob for ever; and of his kingdom there shall be no end."

Christ Jesus is both the humble carpenter—son of Mary, and the coming King who will reign over all of God's creation!

Messiah was to have a double anointing—a ministry of mercy as a Savior—a ministry of judgment, as a coming King to sit on David's throne. Jesus came at his first advent to suffer for the sins of the people, and his role as Judge and King will be fulfilled at his second advent. The prophets were unable to distinguish between these two advents. Isaiah 61·1-2 is an illustration of this. Compare this to Luke 4:18-21. While Christ was reading this in Capernaum, he stopped abruptly when he had concluded all of the things that were predicted for his first advent. He made no mention of the remaining things which are to be fulfilled when he comes again. Between "the acceptable year of the Lord" and the "day of vengeance of our God" was a period convering this present church age already over 1,900 years long.

Truly, the Old Testament prophets described the different pictures of the Messiah. They predicted his sufferings on the cross and also his second coming in glory (1 Peter 1:10-11). They wrote as the Spirit directed concerning "the sufferings of Christ and the glory that should follow," but they had no way of knowing the exact time when these things were to be fulfilled, nor could they see that long period (this entire present church age) that was to elapse between the cross and the crown. They saw the two mountain peaks (the cross and the crown), but they did not see the valley in between (the church age). They could not see how Messiah could be a mighty King and also be "cut off" for the sins of the people (Daniel 9:26). The only answer, of course, was by resurrection. In Acts 2:25-32 Peter quotes from Psalm 16:10 and says that David here is speaking of the resurrection of Christ. Then he added, "This Jesus hath God raised up, whereof we are all witnesses." According to Old Testament prophecy, Christ was to come both as a sacrificial lamb and as a conquering lion of the tribe of Judah. So there was perplexity in the minds of the Old Testament prophets as to the "manner of time" when all this would be fulfilled. But we stand on this side of Calvary and can readily separate the fulfilled prophecies of the "first advent" from the unfulfilled prophecies of the "second advent."

Not only a Savior from our sins but also God has prophesied he will send a King, and this King will set up a Kingdom on this earth. He will execute judgment in the earth (Jeremiah 23:5). Jesus was the promised "son of David" who is to reign on David's throne. But Jesus was rejected at his first coming and was crucified. He arose from the dead. He now sits at the right hand of the Father. What about the kingdom that was offered? It has been postponed. The "Throne of David" will be given to Christ (Acts 15:13-18).

Daniel gives us a picture of what will happen to "the kings of the earth" and their kingdoms when Jesus comes back. In

Daniel 2, he outlines Gentile dominion, beginning with the Babylonian Empire under King Nebuchadnezzar, and ending with the revived Roman Empire just prior to our Lord's return. History has seen the fourth kingdom of "the iron rule" divided into two parts. This is typified by the two legs of the image, symbolic of the eastern and western divisions of the Roman Empire. But the last stage of that kingdom is yet to be fulfilled as foreshadowed by the ten toes of the image. The ten kings representing the last form of world power and empire will give allegiance to the Antichrist. He will be the head of this confederacy of nations. "And in the days of these kings shall the God of heaven set up a kingdom, which shall never be destroyed" (Daniel 2:43-44). As Daniel beheld the vision, he saw the stone smite "the image upon his feet." The Lord Jesus is the smiting "stone . . . cut out of the mountain without hands." Scripture often refers to Christ as a "Stone" (1 Corinthians 10:4, Psalm 118:22). Christ was also the foundation stone of the church (Matthew 16:18). So Christ, as the smiting stone, will put an end to Gentile world power when he comes in glory to reign. His kingdom, as a mountain, shall fill the earth.

When Jesus returns to earth, he will bring his saints with him. Gentile dominion will come to an end, and God's chosen people, Israel, will receive Jesus as their Messiah and King. God will fulfill his covenant with Abraham and David, as he said he would. After the seventieth week of Daniel has come to an end, Jesus will come in glory to reign on this earth. "His feet will stand in that day on the Mount of Olives" (Zechariah 14:4). In Acts 1 we read that he ascended from the Mount of Olives:

"And while they looked stedfastly toward heaven as he went up, behold, two men stood by them in white apparel; Which also said, Ye men of Galilee, why stand ye gazing up into heaven? this same Jesus, which is taken up from you into heaven, shall so come in like manner as ye have seen him go into heaven" (Acts 1:10-11).

Our Lord Jesus Christ is a coming King. He is the true son
of David. No other since the first Christian century could establish such a claim. Through Mary, Jesus obtained his literal
descent from King David. From Mary's marriage to Joseph (who
was also a "son of David"), he obtained his legal right to David's
throne. Mary was Joseph's wife before Jesus was born and this
made Joseph Jesus' legal father—his foster father. So, through
all of this we see Jesus' right to be a king and sit on a throne.
Until Jesus' rejection as king, there were preserved in the Temple
all genealogical records, but when Jerusalem and the Temple
were destroyed in 70 A.D. the records were destroyed. All we
can ever possess of the genealogical tables are those of Matthew
and Luke to give us the lineal descent of the Messiah from
King David. But Jesus is truly that King. In Psalm 2 we see
the coronation of Messiah as King on Mount Zion (verse 6).
In Psalm 47 we see Messiah as God and his coronation as King
of the earth (verses 2, 7). Psalm 72 gives us the most complete
picture in the book of Psalms of Messiah's coming Kingdom
and his reign of righteousness.

As the Lord Jesus after his resurrection appeared personally
to his brother James, and through him won all his brethren
to the faith, and as the Lord personally appeared to Saul on
the road to Damascus, so the coming Lord will appear to his
brethren, the people of Israel, and win them to himself as their
Messiah and Savior.

"And one shall say unto him, What are these wounds
in thine hands? Then he shall answer, Those with which
I was wounded in the house of my friends" (Zechariah
13:6).

". . . and they shall look upon me whom they have
pierced, and they shall mourn for him, as one mourneth

for his only son, and shall be in bitterness for him, as one that is in bitterness for his firstborn" (Zechariah 12:10).

The fifty-third chapter of Isaiah will be the prayer of penitent Israel in that day. When Jesus returns to earth he will return in great power and glory, but Israel will look back to Calvary and see that she crucified her Savior. She will mourn for him and say:

"He is despised and rejected of men; a man of sorrows, and acquainted with grief: and we hid as it were our faces from him; he was despised, and we esteemed him not.

"Surely he hath borne our griefs, and carried our sorrows: yet we did esteem him stricken, smitten of God, and afflicted.

"But he was wounded for our transgressions, he was bruised for our iniquities: the chastisement of our peace was upon him; and with his stripes we are healed" (Isaiah 53:3-5).

Happy day, glorious day, when Israel receives her King!

As the Old Testament closes with the expectation unrealized concerning the coming of Israel's King and his Kingdom, so the New Testament opens with the advent of the King and the offer of his Kingdom to the nation of Israel. He came the first time 2,000 years ago, according to the promise of the Old Testament, and he is coming again some day, according to the promise of both the Old and New Testaments. We cannot know the day or the hour, and we would not for a moment try to set dates (Acts 1:6-7). All the date-setters of the past have proved to be false prophets. In Matthew 24:36 Jesus said, "But of the day and hour knoweth no man, no, not the angels of heaven, but my Father only." But he is surely coming! Jesus of Nazareth has fulfilled and will fulfill every requirement of prophecy concerning the Messiah.

When Jesus came the first time, his coming had been so specifically foretold that we wonder why people failed to recognize him. Jesus came into the world with so many identification tags on him that it seems no one could have failed to recognize him as the promised Messiah. His coming was the theme of all the Old Testament prophecies, and the theologians of that day should have recognized him. Yet, when he came, they missed him completely. In addition to all the identification marks, he came also with signs and wonders and miracles, to prove that he was the promised Messiah. He healed the sick, cleansed the lepers, cast out demons, walked on the water, raised the dead, and gave a thousand other evidences that he was the "one who was to come." But they would not believe on him. The theologians came asking for a sign from heaven. Jesus refused them, and castigated them for not being able to recognize him (Matthew 16:1-3). *But this same Jesus who came that long ago is coming back again.* He is now seated at the right hand of the Father waiting to return. No one who takes his Bible seriously can doubt the return of the Lord Jesus Christ. His Second Coming is mentioned 240 times in the New Testament alone. There is no truth more certain in the entire Bible than the personal, literal, and imminent return of the Lord Jesus Christ to this earth.

There are over 300 predictions in the Old Testament concerning the coming Messiah, and Christ Jesus will fulfill them all. Because the Scriptures of the first coming have been fulfilled, we know the prophecies concerning the second coming will also be fulfilled. As the first coming of the Christ into the world nearly 2,000 years ago covered a period of time—from Bethlehem to Calvary—so also will his second coming cover a period of time—from the translation of the church to his return in glory with the church to establish his millennial Kingdom in the earth. During this brief period there will take place an earthly and a heavenly scene. While the Judgment Seat of Christ and the Marriage of the Lamb are taking place in heaven, the seventieth week of Daniel will be running its course on earth. This is called the tribulation period which is described in Revelation chapters 6-18.

Will God deliver his people from this terrible judgment which is to come upon all the world? Yes. Gloriously, triumphantly, yes!

The personal return of the Son of God from heaven is the hope of the believer, and it is for us to study and search the Scriptures concerning this great event, and to find therein the words of the prophets of the Old Testament, the testimony of the Lord Jesus Christ himself, and the words of his apostles inspired by the Holy Spirit. Then may he who walked with the two on the Emmaus road, expounding to them "in all the scriptures the things concerning himself" causing their hearts to burn within them, draw near to us and so speak to us that our yearning cry shall henceforth be, "Come, Lord Jesus."

PART II

THE HEAVENLY MANDATE, AND THE EARTHLY ASSIGNMENT

[WORK]

"Occupy till I come."

Luke 19:13

"And the gospel of the kingdom shall be preached in all the world for a witness unto all nations; and then shall the end come."

Matthew 24:14

"And he said unto them, It is not for you to know the times or the seasons, which the Father hath put in his own power. But ye shall receive power, after that the Holy Ghost is come upon you: and ye shall be witnesses unto me both in Jerusalem, and in all Judaea, and in Samaria, and unto the uttermost part of the earth."

Acts 1:7-8

TO THE WORK!

To the work! to the work! we are servants of God,
Let us follow the path that our Master has trod;
With the balm of His counsel our strength to renew,
Let us do with our might what our hands find to do.

To the work! to the work! there is labor for all;
For the kingdom of darkness and error shall fall;
And the name of Jehovah exalted shall be,
In the loud swelling chorus, "Salvation is free!"

To the work! to the work! in the strength of the Lord,
And a robe and a crown shall our labor reward,
When the home of the faithful our dwelling shall be,
And we shout with the ransomed, "Salvation is free!"

FANNY J. CROSBY (1820-1915)

1
The Evangelization of the World

But ye shall receive power, after that the Holy Ghost is come upon you: and ye shall be witnesses unto me both in Jerusalem, and in all Judaea, and in Samaria, and unto the uttermost part of the earth. (Acts 1:8).

Then the eleven disciples went away into Galilee, into a mountain where Jesus had appointed them. And when they saw him, they worshipped him: but some doubted. And Jesus came and spake unto them, saying, All power is given unto me in heaven and in earth. Go ye therefore, and teach all nations, baptizing them in the name of the Father, and of the Son, and of the Holy Ghost: Teaching them to observe all things whatsoever I have commanded you: and, lo, I am with you alway, even unto the end of the world. Amen.
(Matthew 28:16-20).

Picture the entire world as proportionally reduced to a village of only 1,000 people. Can you feature the composition of that hamlet? Sixty of them would be Americans, and 940 would be from other nations. But the sixty Americans would control just over half of the total income of the village. The 940 representatives from other geographical areas would work just as hard, yet make less than half the income of the sixty. Of the total, only 303 would be white, 697 of various other pigmentations. The sixty Americans could all reasonably expect to reach seventy years, but the remaining 940 would have only fatuous desires for forty years. The lowest income of the sixty Americans would be higher than the average of the rest. Half of the 940 would

49

be illiterate, neither able to read nor to write. Still more alarming is that half of the village would know of Karl Marx, and many would live under and honor some form of Communist ideology. On the other hand, less than half of the village would have heard about Jesus Christ, and few of that number would know him personally.

About 1,940 years ago Jesus enunciated his commission —Jerusalem, Judaea, Samaria, the world! But in many respects the world was more nearly covered with the gospel by the end of the first century than today. This is true in spite of the fact that those early Christians owned no church properties, had no mission boards, labored in daily danger of the confiscation of what limited possessions they counted their own, and often despaired of life itself. By contrast, we are a part of a nation of vast wealth and eminent success. Churches abound, resources and personnel abound for the accomplishment of Christ's com- mission. Though much has been courageously, skillfully, and often adventurously attained in world missions, the unfinished task grows larger every minute. New babies are born around the clock. We need to reassess our missions program until Jesus comes back.

The Need for Christian Compassion

Numerous factors ought to motivate renewed zeal in mission involvement. Second Corinthians 5 introduces the rationale for the missionary enterprise in terms of a knowledge concerning "the terror of the Lord" which results in a persuasive effort on the part of the disciple. A higher plane is achieved when the apostle to the Gentiles points to the love of Christ as the ultimate constraining force. This latter exercise of love can be viewed lucidly in the life of Jesus and ought to be duplicated in our lives. His altruistic endeavors unfolded as natural blossoms from the love of his heart.

No clearer view of the compassion of the Christ can be found than when the Eternal King laments the fate of the city of Jerusalem. The pathos, the tenderness, the ubiquitous love of our Lord pour forth like a torrent as he speaks of his desire to harbor Jerusalem's inhabitants. Again, Jesus is moved with compassion as he sees the multitudes as sheep void of shepherds. The reactions of Americans in the Orient are instructive. The average tourist is alternately amazed, amused, or frustrated by the throngs. How often have I watched believers with tears welling up in their eyes as they behold the multitude of the confused. That is the difference. To some, the Oriental hordes are just surplus people, population explosion problems, more mouths to feed. But the Christian must view them through the eyes of Jesus. He must see them as lovely men for whom Christ died.

What is it that produces Christian compassion? I believe there are several inducements.

(1) Cognizance of lostness. No believer genuinely aware of what it means to be lost and observant of the destitution of the human dilemma should lack compassion. When the believer also comprehends the richness of life and prosperity of spirit which it is God's desire to bestow, spiritual illness and divine remedy in contrast ought to radically spur our compassion. A productive exercise for any believer would be contemplation of what it means to be lost. Lostness involves danger, impending disaster, loneliness, confusion, and inadequacy.

(2) Recognition of the price of atonement. When it first dawns on the human consciousness how great was the sacrifice of Jesus, one cannot help being overcome. Jesus is said to have "emptied" himself. The king became a servamt—the prince became a pauper. In agony, a sinless, stainless, spotless Lamb of God accepted vicariously the vilest and most vicious of man's crimes and paid for them at Calvary. How could such knowledge fail to produce compassion?

(3) The nature of hell. I still believe in a darkened, lonely,

tragic place called hell. I do not purport to understand it. But the Book teaches it, and I know that somehow, in the divine economy, men who refuse Christ here will spend eternity shamefully and horribly separated from God and from every flaunted expression of his grace. Not even my most verbose antagonist do I wish to see in hell. Knowing about hell should make us love men.

(4) The nature of heaven. The contrast between the horrors of hell and the haven of heaven is the difference between the East and the West, between noonday and midnight. A heaven of continuing responsibilities free from error and weariness, and an eternally fresh experience of worship and fellowship with the living Lord, blend together as an eternal source of compassion for lost men.

There is a dear woman in Dallas who exemplifies the spirit of compassion which ought to be the property of every believer. When in the process of the evening, the news special depicts in sight and sound the plight of the hungry, the war-torn, the poor, the lost—this saint of our Lord cannot watch with customary detachment. To one watching her eyes it becomes apparent that she feels with the sufferer. Soon tears flow and before the time has passed, she may be found on her face before God in behalf of the lost of her globe. Until Jesus comes back, compassion for the lost of the whole world must be part and parcel of our calling.

The Need for Intercessory Prayer

We have arrived at an awesome day in which our people have transferred the works of God to the actions of men. We respond to the mission plea with our best energies and our largest gifts, and we provide at least lip service to the devotion of prayer. But our lives are not lives bathed in supplication to the Lord for the missionary enterprise.

There is a most amazing story that I have come across concerning Samuel Morris, the little African boy miraculously delivered out of the hand of his captors just before being murdered on the Dark Continent. After Samuel's conversion he came to our shores to study. During the few short years before his untimely death, Samuel was invited by churches to come and pray the way we ask men today to come and preach. Can you imagine a boy so powerful in prayer, so profound in intercession, that churches were immersed in genuine revival when he stood in the pulpit and prayed? Can you fathom the mystery of a little black boy walking so closely with God that heaven came down and was attendant upon his every word?

Perhaps more than anything else our churches and our people need to master the communicative process which we call prayer. Countries are rapidly closing. What more can we do for Cambodia and South Viet Nam? We are reduced to prayer! But alas, that is like saying to a soldier, "You are reduced only to an atomic bomb." Stripped of many other weapons in our missionary arsenal, we still have the most powerful one at our disposal. Until Jesus comes back we must insert our souls into the missionary task in prayer.

That prayer should be of two varieties. (1) Jesus taught that the harvest was ready, but the laborers were too few. He explicitly said that his disciples were to pray for laborers to be sent forth. Yet, it is a curiosity that all across our land there are churches undisturbed by the fact that no one has gone from their fellowship as a preacher or missionary. This abnormal state has existed for so long that it is mistaken for normalcy. Few pray that laborers will be sent. (2) Then we are to pray for the conversion of the multitudes. Christ spent the early hours of the morning alone with the Father. He was able to say to Peter on one crisis occasion, "I have prayed for you." Jesus prayed specifically and broadly. He prayed for specific individuals. He also prayed for the multitudes. The same practice can be observed in Paul. We can do no less!

A World Mission Strategy

Until Jesus comes back, our strategy for world missions must be bold and pressed to the utmost. We are under such a profound, heavenly mandate to witness to the world concerning the hope we have in Christ Jesus. Do you remember the words of the Lord God to the prophet in Ezekiel 3:17-18?

"Son of man, I have made thee a watchman unto the house of Israel: therefore hear the word at my mouth, and give them warning from me.

When I say unto the wicked, Thou shalt surely die; and thou givest him not warning, nor speakest to warn the wicked from his wicked way, to save his life; the same wicked man shall die in his iniquity; but his blood will I require at thine hand."

That same word is addressed to us today by the Spirit of the Lord. It is a call for lay involvement in an expanded program of missions, as well as a heavy reminder of the all-significant assignment of the career missionary. The vast disproportion between the ratio of population growth and the spiritual birth of new disciples substantiates the necessity for a massive, astro-age response to the evangelistic appeal.

In 1950, with Dr. Duke K. McCall, then executive director of the Executive Committee of the Southern Baptist Convention, I made a mission journey around the world. Upon our return, Dr. E. C. Routh, editor of our foreign missions magazine, *The Commission,* asked me to write an article for the journal giving my impressions of our ministries on the foreign fields. I prayerfully wrote the article. That was a quarter of a century ago. After the passing of the twenty-five years I am still convinced of the truth of the convictions I voiced then.

"On foreign fields above everything else we need to build churches. Our main business is not the school, the hospital, or the dispensing of alms. It is winning the lost to Christ and training the saved in church membership. There are places in this world where the denominations have invested fortunes in the building of institutions of higher learning, and after generations they still have no churches. The people were heathen before the Christian missionary came; the people are merely pagans now with college degrees. There are some areas, even in our Baptist work, where the school is almost everything, and the church is almost nothing.

"We need the school and the Christian teacher, we need the hospital and the Christian doctor, but most of all and above all we need the preacher and the church and the evangelization of the lost. I can show you a country where the denominations have combined to carry on a wonderful institutional program representing millions of invested dollars and untold sacrificial effort. By the side of that combined group is a denomination that refused to enter into the amalgamation and refused to be enticed into the seductive fields of higher education, but stayed by the main business of winning the lost and building the churches. That single denomination with its church-centered program is now larger by far than all those amalgamated groups with their cultural institutions.

"What we want to do is sow the world down with churches preaching the whole gospel of Jesus Christ and winning the lost wherever we can reach the human heart. To do this we must have pastors and Christian workers, and that, of course, calls for schools and seminaries and training centers. But the schools and the seminaries and the training centers are not ends in themselves; they are but adjuncts to the great task of establishing the churches and evangelizing the world. Whether the Indonesian knows the Greek classics or not, and whether or not he adopts Western cultural patterns, is absolutely immaterial so far as I am concerned. But whether he knows our Savior or not is the most vital question in this world and in the world to come.

God help us to help him to Jesus!

"We need to encourage and to help the converts on foreign fields to build sanctuaries of worship that appeal to the finest leaders of the land.

"Go through the towns and cities of Moslem countries. As in Africa, they are building fine, imposing mosques. Go anywhere and everywhere and watch the Roman Catholics, as in Japan. Their church buildings are imposing and in themselves constitute eloquent invitations to join with a group that has come to stay. O Lord, that our Baptist people might be able to build worthy houses of worship! It would pay us a thousandfold to do so.

"I am not ashamed of our little churches and our small, ill-housed congregations, but I am so thankful when I come across a glorious new church building like our First Baptist Church in Hiroshima, Japan, or the Ijaiye Baptist Church in Abeokuta, Nigeria, or the Olivet Baptist Church in Honolulu. It makes a difference—that mosque, that cathedral, or that Baptist church in the big town. If we are to win the people, one marvelous instrument to employ is a beautiful and adequate building. We are not fly-by-nighters who come and go, but solid, substantial Christian citizens who are in the heart of the city for the hearts of the city.

"In my humble judgment, we need to concentrate upon areas that are responsive to the gospel, then with their help, turn our faces unitedly toward the more difficult fields. Some of the British Baptist missionaries of India said to us: 'That great and wise missionary leader. William Carey, made one mistake in his missionary strategy. In his attempt to cover the vast unevangelized areas of the Ganghes he placed his mission stations too far apart. We have struggled to carry them on, but have been forced in sorrow to abandon many of them. They are too isolated and scattered.'

"Our world is so big, and our mission funds and forces are so limited, until it seems to me that we ought not to try to cover a vast territory ineffectively, but we ought to concentrate on those places and people where we have our greatest opportunity and go all-out there to win the people to Christ. There are places in the world where we have a wide open door. The people are hungry to hear the message. They are ready to turn to our Lord and Savior.

"I remember one country where Baptist churches and mission stations already organized are ready to be turned over to us. They beg us to come. Why not enter there with all our strength? If we did so, you might be able to create through them another Southern Baptist Convention which would then help to evangelize the harder and more remote places. The difference between a river and a swamp is that one has banks and the other has not; one tries to spread all over creation, the other follows a channeled course.

"It is a matter of tears and regret that we do not have the funds or the missionaries to go everywhere. Until we are able, let us go where we have the hungry hearts and the open door. Maybe through them God will raise up added helpers to go with us to the more difficult and more unresponsive places.

"One certain strategy that would bless our mission efforts immeasurably is the development of a missionary cadre in all the areas where we work for Jesus. I do not think, even if we had until the end of time, we would ever be able to send out enough missionaries to do all the soul-winning and all the church establishing. If we all went to the foreign fields I do not think we all together could do it. The Africans must evangelize the Africans, the Japanese the Japanese, the Chinese the Chinese.

"What a cadre does in training an army is what our missionaries must do in creating a denomination. The churches must be indigenous if they are to survive, and the leaders must be native if they are to live and grow through the years. We must train them to carry on so that, if we are forced to leave, as in China, the congregations will remain strong and faithful in their witness for Christ.

"Leaders grow by leading. Preachers become real preachers

by preaching. Churches become self-sustaining by assuming responsibility. A denomination becomes effective when it realizes its great destiny and mission in the kingdom of God.

"In this matter of creating indigenous churches our Foreign Mission Board is wise beyond compare. Our leaders in all these things I have mentioned are doing a heroic job. They need our help and our gifts, our love and our prayers to do more."

Mobilization of Our Mission Army

Mobilization of our entire Christian army is an unmitigated necessity if we are to do anything for our world before Jesus comes back. With all of my heart I believe that we can be concerned about numbers (the Holy Spirit evidently felt this concern since he saw fit to record the number saved at Pentecost) without losing our personal involvement with men as individuals. I further maintain that we can produce large numbers of disciples without sacrificing discipleship training, and that we can train men for Christ without sacrificing the evangelization of the multitudes. Until Jesus comes back, we must witness for him around the world.

The year was 1850. Adoniram Judson, our first Baptist missionary from America to Burma, lay at death's door. Death was no stranger; he had been there poised at its brink before. Now this herald of the Lord, this harbinger of the coming Christ, lay again at the entrance to eternity. His missionary labors had brought him the sorrow of burying wife and children in the Burmese soil. Imprisoned in vermin-filled, criminally-controlled camps, he had endured personal torture while harboring his precious translation of the New Testament in the language of the people who now dispensed misery. Those harlequins of justice subjected Judson to tortures of mind that altogether transcended physical suffering.

Nevertheless, Judson labored incessantly, laying the foundation for the church in Burma. In many ways his work in Burma was as effective as the labor of Carey, Marshman, and Ward in India. Now as the evangelist prepared to slip from limitation to ultimate freedom, from terrestial labor to celestial rest, as he prepared to don the garments of immortality, he spoke of his decease. "I go with the joy of a school boy bounding away from school."

I submit that Judson could face his coronation confidently; he could make his entrance to the presence of the King without fear because he knew that he had kept the faith, fought the good fight, finished his course that Christ had given. He was not yet perfect. But his energies had been totally expended in pursuit of the souls of men for the Kingdom of our Lord.

If we would stand without shame before Christ, if our desire is to be ready when the consummation comes, then the missionary task—winning our world for Jesus—must be primary until Jesus comes back.

2
Doing Business for God

Occupy till I come (Luke 19:13).

"Occupy till I come," said Jesus in Luke 19:13. The word "occupy" in English causes such imagery as an "army of occupation" to flash on the screen of one's mind. The command of Christ, to "occupy" till he comes back, does indeed savor of this idea. The total event of his incarnation includes his teachings, his plan for the disciples after he was gone, as well as the events in the drama of redemption toward the end of his earthly ministry.

Much cosmic territory had been conquered by the Lord by the time he stood on Olivet with the disciples just prior to his ascension. The disciples asked, "Lord, dost thou at this time restore the kingdom to Israel?"—a likely query in view of the forty days' display of power in eleven post-resurrection appearances. This question was a built-in reason for Christ's specifying exactly what he wanted his followers to do until he should return. The Christian movement had established a spearhead on the boundary of the territory. The great mandate of immediate conquest quickly followed. The Master said, "And ye shall be witnesses unto me both in Jerusalem, and in all Judaea, and in Samaria, and unto the uttermost part of the earth" (Acts 1:8). The timing of the Lord's return was none of their business. What was their relationship to the enterprise? Simply, without qualification, without subsidiary or secondary functions to hamper them, they were to be "witnesses." Witnesses many of them actually became. The book of Acts, the only literature in the New Testament which spans the gap between the ascension of Christ and the rapidly proliferating churches and Christians throughout the Roman Empire, vividly pictures this action. It is the story of "the occupying" by the early disciples of Christ.

An ever-increasing host of Christians, "gossiping the gospel" as climaxed in the resurrection of Christ, appears throughout the Roman Empire shortly after the ascension. Luke faithfully traces these Christian "flares of illumination" from Jerusalem to Rome. They witnessed to the fulfillment and dramatic realization of "the hope of Israel," or the resurrection. This hope Paul spelled out with increasing specificity. He said before both the Sanhedrin and Felix, "And have hope toward God, which they themselves also allow, that there shall be a resurrection of the dead, both of the just and the unjust" (Acts 24:15). The apostle had already preached before the Jews in Jerusalem, who would have killed him as he stood halfway up the stairs of the tribunal's castle, "touching the resurrection of the dead I am called in question by you this day" (Acts 23:6; 24:15, 21). Governor Festus chafed at the problem of having an uncondemned man in the prison at Caesarea, "But had certain questions against him of their own superstition, and of one Jesus, which was dead, whom Paul affirmed to be alive" (Acts 25:19). Finally, the doughty soldier of the cross affirmed before Governor Festus and visiting King Agrippa:

> "And now I stand and am judged for the hope of the promise made of God unto our fathers: Unto which promise our twelve tribes, instantly serving God day and night, hope to come. For which hope's sake, king Agrippa, I am accused of the Jews. Why should it be thought a thing incredible with you, that God should raise the dead?" (Acts 26:6-8).

These few specific statements make it clear that Christian witnesses were to testify to what they had experienced concerning the living Christ: he who had been crucified was now gloriously alive and reigning in their hearts. They were to witness to this experience unto the uttermost part of the earth. "The uttermost part of the earth" indicates the dimensions of the territory which the first Christians were commanded to "occupy."

The Urgency of the Witnessing Assignment

Christ said, "For unto whomsoever much is given, of him shall be much required . . ." (Luke 12:48b). Our responsibility to "occupy" until Jesus comes back again is nothing short of awesome. Christ holds us responsible. We must give account. Further, the destiny of our fellow human beings is at stake. Jesus said, "And fear not them which kill the body, but are not able to kill the soul: but rather fear him which is able to destroy both soul and body in hell" (Matthew 10:29). That which has the image of Almighty God, the Creator, stamped upon it is indestructible. There is that about man which is immortal, which will last forever.

The most crucial issue confronting us as we contemplate what we should do until Jesus comes back is whether man is composed of a fortuitous combination of molecules and atoms bouncing on the sea of time, only to be lost down the drain of eternity when his sojourn on earth is consummated, or whether man has within him a life of the divine and the eternal which makes him truly worth redeeming. The Christian revelation says that God has decreed that man is worth redeeming. It further makes the assertion that it is unthinkable, tragic, and dreadfully dangerous for a man to miss the mark and in death go out into the great unknown without Christ.

Time is not to go on forever. The assumption that one generation will continue to appear only to be followed by another as the first vanishes, in unending cycles—indefinitely, forever—is not part of the Christian revelation. The truth is, to use a contradiction in terms, that *the time will come when time shall be no more.*

Occasionally it is opined that one has to give up much to be a witnessing Christian. To a degree this is true. When one takes Christ seriously, when a man commits himself to Christ on Christ's terms, he must be willing to forsake mother and father, houses and lands, and everything else in order to be a genuine follower. But one should not think of what he has to give up if he becomes a Christian. Rather should he contemplate what he gets. He receives the joy of a mind at peace with God and his fellowman; he receives infinite rewards and blessings in this life; he receives confidence and assurance about the future.

Yes, it is true that one gives up much as he becomes a Christian. One misses many things in going to heaven. One of them is hell.

> How happy every child of grace,
> Who knows his sins forgiven!
> "This earth," he cries, "is not my place,
> I seek a home in heaven!
>
> "A country far from mortal sight
> Which yet by faith I see,
> The land of rest, the saint's delight,
> The heaven prepared for me."

The danger to those who obey the Lord's injunction to "occupy" is real. As the Lord told the story in Luke 19, an enterprising nobleman went into a far country to receive for himself a kingdom, after which he would return. His order to his stewards was, "Occupy till I come." But this man had enemies: "But his citizens hated him, saying, we will not have this man to reign over us" (Luke 19:14). The witnessing with which Christ commanded the disciples to "occupy" themselves till he comes again has always been opposed vigorously by the forces of evil.

When Christian witnessing is accepted, believed upon, acted upon, many changes occur. Changes in men's personal lives abound. Eventually many men who have been changed by Christ will inaugurate changes in stratification, immoral structures, and improper human relationships. The segments of humanity who do not want these changes, who are not willing as yet to have all men changed and elevated to clean living in Christ, set themselves in array against God and his anointed. But witnessing is to bear fruit. It is to change men, and they in turn ought to change evil structures within the framework of society. Because some evils bring much gain to many others, these others oppose aggressively any movement that would take the lucrative element out of their nefarious business. This causes Christian witnesses oftimes to suffer.

Our Sufferings Completing the Sufferings of Christ

Paul made a puzzling statement in Colossians 1:24. The ASV translates the passage correctly, as well as graphically, "Now I rejoice in my sufferings, and fill up on my part that which is lacking of the afflictions of Christ in my flesh for his body's sake, which is the church." When Paul says that something is "lacking in the afflictions of Christ," one is almost tempted to remonstrate: "What do you mean, Paul? Were Christ's sufferings actually insufficient? Did he not remain on the cross long enough, from 9 A.M. until 3 P.M.? Do you mean that Christ did not suffer enough? Were the nails not long enough? Was the spear thrust into his side not sharp enough? Was the crown of thorns too tender to perforate human flesh?"

Paul would be the first to reply: "No, indeed! I meant no such thing. You have read throughout my writings and elsewhere that when Christ died on the cross, his atoning death was a full, free, final sacrifice for our sins. There is no other possibility of anything other than his death and the shedding of his blood being efficacious for the remission of sins."

"Then, what do you mean, Paul, when you say that there is something lacking in the afflictions of Christ?" Paul rebuts: "I did not say that Christ did not suffer enough. What I did say was that I am supplementing the afflictions of Christ through spreading the news of his offer of full, final, free redemption to all mankind. I am doing it in reckless abandonment. An atonement achieved thus by his great agony must now be announced to all the world. A free pardon procured at so great a cost to the Savior must now be proclaimed to every member of the human race. And some of us are going to suffer doing so. Already I have been shipwrecked thrice, beaten with forty stripes save one on several occasions, stoned and left for dead outside the city of Lystra."

Paul so construed the economy of God that he laid the sufferings of Christ's followers alongside the Lord's own sufferings. Christ's sufferings were those of achieving our forgiveness; our sufferings are those of announcing this fact to an often rebellious world. Christ's agony was that of procuring our salvation by giving his life's blood; ours is that of proclaiming it to a race often unreceptive. In this sense Christians are filling up that with which "is lacking" in the afflictions of Christ.

Christ's afflictions were those of creativity, self-giving, and productivity; ours the price of logistics, marketing, and transportation. Christ has done the work in making redemption possible and in bringing it to a state of absolute consummation—the news of it must now be wafted by human instrumentality to all men. This will involve many in suffering, sacrifice, and pain.

One Christian, as he neared the end of his period of "occupying" for Christ, said, "I have fought a good fight."

Christians cannot afford to forget what they are here for. Christ has commanded them to "occupy" until he comes back. This will involve struggles and battles. The figure of a soldier is not inappropriate in referring to the serious Christian. "By faith Abraham, when he was called to go out unto a place which he should after receive for an inheritance, obeyed; and he went

out not knowing whither he went" (Hebrews 11:8, ASV). Rich
in possessions, friends, and loved ones, Abraham answered God's
call to leave Mesopotamia and proceed to Palestine. Apparently
he had never been there. It was not certain that he could "make
good" in that land afflicted with intermittent famines and inhab-
ited by warlike peoples. His was an act of faith of the highest
order. By faith, he was willing to sojourn in a strange land.

Abraham engaged in literal battles in order to fulfill the
mystical mission on which God had sent him. On one occasion
Abraham took 318 of his "trained servants" (undershepherds);
he pursued the vicious kings, who had abducted his nephew
Lot, all the way to the Damascus area. He did battle with them
and returned with Lot, Lot's family, and much booty. He pro-
ceeded to tithe the spoils taken after the battle. The Holy Scriptures are careful to record faithful Abraham in practice of this
sacred obligation toward his God. Such "lesser" things are as
such a part of our "occupational" responsibilities while ap-
proaching the end-time as vocalizing our testimony.

Without complaining, Abraham trustingly obeyed God. Faith
induces the willingness to do God's will. His purpose is best
fulfilled within us sometimes by blind obedience in what may
seem to be an unreasonable request. Abraham would be safer
within the circle of God's will among warlike tribes than he
would be among the comforts of his homeland and people, yet
outside God's will. So reason our loyal missionaries. By faith
they go out to do God's bidding in the "regions beyond," and
their radiance bespeaks a greater joy than most other Christians
know. Our support makes possible for them to proclaim the
gospel overseas. They indeed continue to "occupy" until Jesus
comes back.

As a soldier of the Lord, Abraham would be the first to gain
a spearhead in the promised land. If there were battles to be
fought, he would be fighting for his God. That is what he was
here for—to fight God's battles regardless of geographical loca-
tion. As he went out, he did not know "whither" but he knew

"why."

Christians are here to fight God's battles. This is a salient feature of the command to "occupy" until the Lord returns. The willingness to take a dangerous post, to go on a daring mission is always evident in hearts aglow with faith. The sense of mission in soldiers of the divine army will not permit the question "Where?"—only "Why?"

The End-time Toward Which All History Is Moving

Christ's second coming is to his first coming what his resurrection was to his death. If Christ had not risen from the grave, we would never have known whether his death dealt efficaciously and efficiently with sin. The chief fruit of sin is death. Therefore, when Christ rose from the grave, his resurrection forever demonstrated that he had conquered our last enemy. This confirmed the power of his death, the power of the blood which symbolizes the giving of his life, and the power of divine forgiveness to those who accept his offering of himself for sin. New life, changed men, and elevated specimens of humanity are the result of his death for sin. Just as his death without his resurrection would be incomplete, it would be illogical to an equal degree, should there be no "eschaton" toward which history is moving. There is an end time. There is a "great and notable day" (Acts 2:20) toward which history is moving.

The alternative to such a climactic consummation of the kingdom of God is a picture of one generation being born, living awhile, and then vanishing from the earth only to make room for another generation now appearing. The solution to the puzzle of life and history is seen in the purposiveness of it all. A purposive principle pervades all Scripture. The word denotes "objective," "teleology," "goal." God was not merely playing with mud when he made man. He created the race for a specific purpose; namely, to glorify His name and to rejoice in His goodness.

Investing in God's Business for Eternal Rewards

The word "occupy" is in the middle voice in its verbal form.
It is *pragmateuomai,* whence our "pragmatic." This is a verb
of action and achievement. It means "to be occupied in anything;
to carry on a business . . . to carry on the business of a banker
or trader" (*Thayer,* page 534). The middle voice brings to the
foreground the fact that responsibility for "occupying" is intensely personal. This reveals the serious responsibility which
each individual Christian has. He is to activate himself in that
enterprise called the Kingdom of God by doing precisely what
Christ has commanded. To carry on the business of the Lord
is headed up primarily in witnessing. But this also involves the
total life of man. His entire spectrum of activity must reflect
the objective of witnessing as being his primary concern.

A question from the lips of Christ may help motivate the
Christian in carrying out the responsibility of witnessing till Jesus
comes back. He said, "For what shall it profit a man, if he shall
gain the whole world and lose his own soul?" (Mark 8:36). To
"occupy" partakes heavily of transacting business in civilian life.
What Christ asks here in Mark 8:36 might be called his "business
text" or the text for the "businessman." If Christianity sometimes
seems idealistic, let it be remembered that Christ always kept
his feet on the ground, even when his head appeared to be
in the clouds. While "good business may not always be good
religion, good religion is always good business." "For what shall
it profit a man, if he shall gain the whole world and lose his
own soul?" This text speaks of "profit," "loss," and "gain." It
is "strictly business." It is as though the Lord were saying, "Come
now, let's get down to business; be practical, be realistic." Is
it good business if those who have negotiated with God in Christ
for peace and forgiveness should neglect to witness to others
about their salvation? "What has a man profited if he shall
gain the whole world and lose his own soul?"

The logic of making every effort to "occupy" until Jesus comes back is seen further in the safety and abiding quality of one's investment. The man who invests in the Kingdom of Christ continues to draw dividends throughout eternity. The greatest yield from his spiritual investment begins to spiral in great proportions only at the time of the return of Christ. The yield reaches even greater climax with the Christian's resurrection and the fruits of his influence on others as long as time shall last. While he is alive he can say, "For me to live is Christ." This is the height scaled by believing men who have taken Christ as Redeemer and Lord. They live with reckless abandon. They are not as concerned with what society thinks of them as they are with pleasing Him who "enrolled them" as His soldiers and stewards. They know that long after life on earth ends they will continue to reap dividends from their investment in Christian living. Land values may fluctuate; stock markets may rise and fall; economic crises may beset the nation. The man who casts his all with Christ Jesus is investing in the one business the success of which is underwritten by the Creator. Men may sometimes feel like they are failing as Christians. However, they would do well to ponder the statement of Woodrow Wilson in about 1922 when he said: "I would rather fail in a movement that will ultimately succeed than to succeed in a movement that will ultimately fail."

Investing in Christian endeavor brings dividends forever. Even in this life we sometimes see the bountiful returns of what is done for Christ.

An American pastor was privileged to preach in the Colaba Baptist Church of Bombay, India, in January, 1941. The English pastor, Reverend Stone, baptized an Indian woman at the close of the service. The American encouraged him, "Congratulations on the baptism of your convert tonight."

"She is not my convert, friend. She is Adoniram Judson's," came the reply.

"But Judson lived over a hundred years ago, more than one thousand miles away from here in the country of Burma," the

American remonstrated.

"True, but the woman whom I baptized tonight fell into the company of some women from that city in Burma in which Judson did so much intense suffering last century. You recall how he was in prison, physically harmed, placed on a starvation diet, and in general persecuted almost beyond description? Well, these women are descendants of people who were influenced by the incomparable life and outstanding witnessing of Adoniram Judson in that city last century. The woman whom I baptized tonight fell into their company as a seamstress, and after a few days she herself became a believer. You see—she is Judson's convert."

Over a hundred years ago! More than one thousand miles away! Yet the work of Judson was still bearing fruit through the descendants of those whom he had led to Christ. The story of his life by Honore Wills Morrow under the title, *The Splendor of God,* still thrills readers with the dramatic account of one of the most noble lives ever lived under the banner of Jesus Christ. Over a century after this man's death, his fruit was still proliferating. Such events but confirm the permanent profits, the safety of the investment, and the abiding dividends for those who are committed to doing what Jesus commanded us to do until he comes back. The Kingdom of Christ is still the best investment of all time, and logically so.

Let us do business for God "till he comes."

3
The Pedagogical Imperative

Thou therefore, my son, be strong in the grace that is in Christ Jesus. And the things that thou hast heard of me among many witnesses, the same commit thou to faithful men who shall be able to teach others also (2 Timothy 2:1-2).

Until the Lord comes back, teach them, educate them, train them! So said Jesus. So said Paul. So would say every discerning leader in the Christian faith. It will be done either by us in the love of the Lord or by them in the world of unbelief. The ways of the world, the streets of the city offer no degrees, confer no diplomas, but they educate with terrible precision. If we have a people of the Lord prepared for his coming, ready to receive the heavenly King, we must be true to the commission of the Lord Jesus to evangelize and to teach. Obedience to the Great Commission carries with it the pedagogical imperative. If God has spoken, then obedience becomes the very highest order of intelligent acting. We bring glory to God when we obey him ourselves; we bring more glory to God when we teach others to obey him.

Loving the Lord Means Teaching His People

Do you remember this story in the last chapter of the gospel of John?

"So when they had dined, Jesus saith to Simon Peter,

Simon, son of Jonas, lovest thou me more than these? He saith unto him, Yea, Lord; thou knowest that I love thee. He saith unto him, Feed my lambs. He saith to him again the second time, Simon, son of Jonas, lovest thou me? He saith unto him, Yea, Lord; thou knowest that I love thee. He saith unto him, Feed my sheep. He saith unto him the third time, Simon, son of Jonas, lovest thou me? Peter was grieved because he said unto him the third time, Lovest thou me? And he said unto him, Lord, thou knowest all things; thou knowest that I love thee. Jesus saith unto him, Feed my sheep" (John 21:15-17).

The meaning is inescapable. We show our love for Christ when we feed his sheep, including his little lambs.

The diet is likewise spelled out by Peter himself: "As newborn babes, desire the sincere milk of the word, that ye may grow thereby" (1 Peter 2:2).

It is easy for us to be critical of the non-evangelical denomination with little or no emphasis on making converts. A concomitant criticism might be justly leveled at some of us: we are zealous to make converts, but our emphasis on the new birth has often left us with a congregation of babies whom we never bring to spiritual maturity. If our people were organized on the basis of spiritual maturity instead of chronological age, we might find our nursery and preschool divisions overloaded with very little need for any adult divisions.

The aim for every new-born child of God is that he grow up. Nothing is sweeter than a new-born babe; nothing brings more grief and heartache to parents than the initial realization that a retarded child can never grow up. Surely our local congregations of spiritual pygmies must bring untold grief to the heart of our heavenly Father.

In delineating the purpose of spiritual gifts, Paul writes in Ephesians 4:13 that apostles, prophets, evangelists, pastors, and teachers are specifically given to educate, and thereby mature the saints. *The Living Bible* translates the passage like this:

> "Why is it that he gives us these special abilities to do certain things best? It is that God's people will be equipped to do better work for him, building up the church, the body of Christ, to a position of strength and maturity; until finally we all believe alike about our salvation and about our Saviour, God's Son, and all become full-grown in the Lord—yes, to the point of being filled full with Christ.
>
> "Then we will no longer be like children, forever changing our minds about what we believe because someone has told us something different, or has cleverly lied to us and made the lie sound like the truth.
>
> "Instead, we will lovingly follow the truth at all times—speaking truly, dealing truly, living truly—and so become more and more in every way like Christ who is the Head of his body, the church. Under his direction the whole body is fitted together perfectly, and each part in its own special way helps the other parts, so that the whole body is healthy and growing and full of love" (Ephesians 4:12-16).

Because of the inevitable rise of false doctrine in the church, Paul had earlier admonished Timothy:

> "Teach these things and make sure everyone learns them well. Don't let anyone think little of you because you are young. Be their ideal; let them follow the way you teach and live; be a pattern for them in your love, your faith, and your clean thoughts. Until I get there, read and explain the Scriptures to the church; preach God's Word" (1 Timothy 4:11-13, TLB).

For these reasons, every church ought to be committed to the business of educating our people through a teaching ministry, whose textbook is the infallible, inerrant Word of God. The emphasis ought always to be on the *exposition, interpretation,* and *application* of the Scriptures, with concomitant results ranging from the small child's exuberant, "He is risen!" on an Easter morning, to the teen-age Chapel Choir's ringing affirmation of "He is alive and I love Him!" in a *Celebrate Life* production, to the majestic "I Know That My Redeemer Liveth" of Handel's *Messiah* from the Sanctuary Choir, to a scholarly dissertation on the implications of the resurrection for our more advanced students in our higher institutions of learning.

We are persuaded that the human body cannot assimilate food it has never eaten; likewise, the believer in Christ remains anemic, undernourished, and even sickly and diseased when he is not given Scriptural food to assimilate for his proper spiritual growth—the milk and meat of the Word. Small wonder that he remains a babe, completely self-centered, whimsical, capricious, and experience-oriented rather than Scripture-oriented. Indeed, his entire relationship with God rests, not upon the finished work of Christ, but rather upon his own emotional condition for the day. Instead of being rooted and grounded in Christ, he is the double-minded man, the spiritually poverty-stricken man, unstable in all his ways, described by James in James 1:8. Emotion has always had a legitimate place in the Christian faith; but it ought to be the frosting on the cake, not the foundation for the edifice. No wonder the Lord told Peter that the great demonstration of his love could be practically manifested in the feeding of his sheep.

Employing Every Means to Mediate the Mind of Christ

But the practical queries ensue: What do we teach? And where? And how? And to whom? And by whom? And on what level? The answer is patently obvious. We ought to teach God's Word to all who will listen—in Sunday School and Training Union, by radio and television, in home Bible classes and WMU, in Vacation Bible Schools and in missions, all over the city and all over the world, by the printed and preached and sung Word, on retreats and in our church school, on choir tours and in civic auditoriums. Wherever there are people for whom Christ died and at whatever level we find them in their understanding, we ought to teach the unsearchable riches of Christ. From the time an infant is brought to us, through the years when we minister to our aged in rest homes and hospitals, the emphasis is always the same: the incarnate, crucified, buried, resurrected, ascended, soon-coming Christ, God's remedy for man's every problem in this world and in the world to come. With special emphasis on the infallibility of the Scripture, the love of God, the atonement of Christ, the centrality of the fact of the resurrection, and the imminent return of the Lord, let us teach with the assurance of God's provision for man's salvation from the penalty, power, and finally the very presence of sin. Let us seek to evoke proper responses from believers with regard to their love both for Christ and his body, the church, with a concomitant proper stewardship of time, talent, and money, as well as a concern for every man as one for whom Christ died. These great foundational truths may be adapted to a "milk" or "meat" mentality and maturity; but when the Spirit of God acts upon the Word of God, the results are inevitable, whether at a choir concert, in a class of young boys, or when the leaders gather on Wednesday night to hear the pastor teach the teachers to prepare themselves to be able to feed the flock.

Our people are bombarded on every side—from without and from within—with subtle, sophisticated, appealing philosophies and philosophers whose pronouncements are directly contrary to God's teachings. More than ever, we need an intellectual basis for our faith and the firm assurance that it is, above all things, *reasonable* to be a Christian. In contemporary art, literature, music, philosophy, and entertainment (as well as in the world of religion) the guiding principles and basic premises either completely ignore or make a travesty of the Christian faith. A popular comedian joked on a recent record, "I was a Southern Democrat and a Southern Baptist until I learned to read and write." The evangelical preacher in the cinema is either an Elmer Gantry or a Marjoe, either hypocritical, dishonest, and lustful, or else incredibly naive and ignorant—always in contradistinction to the sage and kindly village atheist. The implication is clear: the Christian faith is for those who have assassinated their brains, clearly overlooking the facts that the human architects of much of the Old and New Testaments, Moses and Paul, were the brilliantly educated, intellectual giants of their days.

The following advertisements ran in local newspapers. Look at this one.

IS EASTER EMBARRASSING?

It should be. The resurrection rumors once plausible are incredible today. Open questioning is more important than conforming to antiquated creeds.

And again look at this one.

WHAT SHOULD CHILDREN
BE TAUGHT IN SUNDAY SCHOOL?

That God created the world in six days? That man is not a creature of evolution? That Jesus was virgin-born, did miracles, and was literally raised from the dead? That Jesus may come down from the sky just any day now? That only those who believe such assertions with all their hearts are saved while everybody else will burn forever in hell? OR that creation should be studied from all the world's religious views, plus the views of modern science. That man has evolved from a wonderful evolutionary process, and is part and product of nature. That Jesus was most likely a good man who taught many good things, and like many of the religious leaders of the world had myths invented about him by his followers. That religion should deal in the here and now with complete trust in the forces that brought us into existence without morbid fear of death.

A child exposed to this is brought to believe that he is nothing but an animal. If he acts like one, is it any marvel? Our carnal natures makes it much easier for us to believe a lie, which leaves us smug and comfortable, than to believe God's truth, with its awesome demands. Until our people are aware of the nature of human nature as set forth in the Scripture and documented experientially by any honest and inquiring mind, the satanic propaganda that permeates this age may overwhelm us.

The unbridled rise in public education of Marxism, Darwinism, occultism, and secularism reinforces Paul's warnings to his young son in the faith, and is no less applicable to us:

"In fact, evil men and false teachers will become worse and worse, deceiving many, they themselves having been deceived by Satan. But you must keep on believing the things you have been taught. You know they are true for you know that you can trust those of us who have taught you. You know how, when you were a small child, you were taught the holy Scriptures; and it is these that make you wise to accept God's salvation by trusting in Christ Jesus. The whole Bible was given to us by inspiration from God and is useful to teach us what is true and to make us realize what is wrong in our lives; it straightens us out and helps us do what is right. It is God's way of making us well prepared at every point, fully equipped to do good to everyone" (2 Timothy 3:13-17, TLB).

The Tragic Dilemma of the Christian Public School Teacher

Consider the frustration of the public school teacher who works all day in an atmosphere where the name of Christ is either outlawed, ignored, or blasphemed. The first principal of our Dallas First Baptist School placed these words of explanation in our church newspaper, *The Reminder:*

WHO WILL TEACH YOUR CHILDREN?

I want someone to teach my children mathematics who will not forget to suggest to them two dimensions that are frequently forgotten, the brevity of time and the length of eternity. I want someone to teach my children botany who knows how to analyze and classify flowers, and yet I want him by precept and example to point them to One who said, "Consider the lilies of the field." I want someone to teach my children astronomy who will not hesitate to tell them, "The heavens declare the glory of God." I want someone to teach my children rhetoric who knows and uses correct language but one, too, who knows and serves the One who "spake as never man spake." I want someone to teach my children biology who would not think it out of place to quietly, sincerely remind them that "the blood of Jesus Christ, His Son, cleanseth us from all sin."

In the year 1850, Horace Mann, who did not believe Christ was divine, urged the United States Congress to set up a system of free education. He based his desire on the belief that this would save so much tax money. That belief, in turn, was based on his belief that "education" would make society so wise and good that our entire penal system would cease to be needed: jails, constables, sheriffs, judges, policemen, et al.

If Mr. Mann should awaken today he would be quite a green-horn! Statisticians say the current national bill for education is our largest single expense, and alongside that figure is the fact that we cannot furnish sufficient space in jails and prisons to care for all our criminals.

His mistake was not in wanting public school education, but in thinking:

(1) Human nature is essentially good (therefore man needs no Redeemer).
(2) Man is only an animal (has no soul).
(3) Man is supreme (there is no Higher Power).
(4) The will of the group determines moral standards (no responsibility to God).
(5) Crime is caused by anti-social tendencies (not by sin).
(6) Poor environs lead to improper conduct (guilt is nonexistent).

Mr. Mann was a Unitarian, and based his educational belief on his religious belief. As evangelical Christians we base our educational belief on our religious belief. Woe betide us if we do not act consistently with our belief.

What should we be doing until Jesus comes back again? A significant part of our stewardship responsibility is, therefore, vitally involved with educating our people. This can never be done haphazardly, nonchalantly, or incidentally. While a man does not need a doctoral degree from the seminary to be an effective Christian educator, he does need to meet some definite qualifications, including these:

(1) A full assurance of his own salvation.
(2) A genuine devotion to Christ and His church.
(3) A firm confidence in the power and infallibility of the Bible.
(4) A willingness to spend time in prayer and in intensive Bible study.
(5) A teachable spirit.
(6) A genuine interest in the lives of other people and a firm commitment to the task of bringing them to spiritual maturity.
(7) A preeminent desire, above all else, to please God in everything that he undertakes.

A person may have all of these qualities and still be an effective teacher, but without these qualities, he is certain to be ineffective.

Leslie P. Hill expressed the sentiments of many a teacher in this little poem:

> Lord, who am I to teach the way
> To little children day by day
> So prone myself to go astray?
>
> I teach them knowledge, but I know
> How faint the flicker and how low
> The candles of my knowledge glow.
>
> I teach them power to will and do,
> But only now to learn anew
> My own great weakness through and through.
>
> Lord, if their guide I still must be,
> Oh, let the little children see
> The teacher leaning hard on Thee.

With the Apostle Paul, we would add, "Not that we are sufficient of ourselves to think any thing as of ourselves; but our sufficiency is of God" (2 Corinthians 3:5). Looking to God, faithful to God, obedient to God, learning from God, waiting for the coming of the Lord—truly this is the pedagogical imperative.

4
Teaching the Philosophies of Men or the Revelation of God

And daily in the temple, and in every house, they ceased not to teach and preach Jesus Christ (Acts 5:42).

And I saw another angel fly in the midst of heaven, having the everlasting gospel to preach unto them that dwell on the earth, and to every nation, and kindred, and tongue, and people,
Saying with a loud voice, Fear God, and give glory to him; for the hour of his judgment is come: and worship him that made heaven, and earth, and the sea, and the foundations of waters (Revelation 14:6-7).

There is a profound reason for the mandate of God that we teach and preach the way of eternal life in Christ Jesus. Outside of him human speculations are barren, sterile, and empty. They lead to nowhere but disappointment and frustration.

In studying different concepts of different men in different ages, one paramount fact is evident: the inconsistency with which the varying philosophers view the nature of man and of God. Whole systems of philosophy negate, in varying degrees, other systems. Brilliant, analytical minds come to completely contradictory conclusions. Careful research and observation establish certain verities which survive for days, years, or decades—even centuries—and are then relegated into such obscurity that man wonders how he could have been so deluded.

The Confusion of Ancient Greek Philosophies

The Greeks were the first to separate philosophy from religion and mythology. In the Greek colonies philosophy had its beginnings in the sixth century B.C. The first Greek philosophers seemed largely concerned with an attempt to uncover the basic principles of their world. Their work was largely an attempt to account for the similarities and differences of things, with much lesser emphasis upon the nature of man.

Thales looked for a basic principle of unity to which all material reality could be reduced. Pythagoras taught that everything man observes appears to be some combination of points, lines, and surfaces—hence mathematical. Heraclitus focused his attention on the empirical fact of change. Parmenides believed that man is the constant victim of sense illusions, and that change is only an illusion. His thought led to pantheism, that everything is simply an aspect of God, who alone is real. Empedocles held that four elements—earth, air, fire, and water—account for all.

At this point philosophy began to develop from a cosmologically-oriented philosophy to an anthropologically-oriented one. Anaxagoras hinted that principle of mind or intelligence has something to do with reality. The Atomists believed that fundamental particles of matter differ only in shape. When they collide by chance, they either stick together (accounting for birth) or break other combinations apart (accounting for destruction). Philosophically, then, man is simply an aggregate union of material particles for whom death is merely absolute dissolution.

Socrates, Plato, and Aristotle presented many dissimilar views regarding the nature of human nature. Socrates believed that man as an essentially rational creature will do right when he knows right. Plato believed that God's love for infinite self-expression is the clue to creation. Aristotle moved life into the hierarchy of the rational forms, the lower admiring the higher.

Among the Sophists and relativists, Protagoras insisted that man is the measure of all things. Automatically, all absolutes are ruled out; science, truth, and ethics accordingly vary with each man and have only subjective status.

When the whole spectrum of Greek philosophy is examined,

studied, discussed, and analyzed, it still leaves us lost and undone. We need a Savior and a Deliverer from our sins and from the judgment of death.

The Impotent Emptiness of Modern Philosophies

Largely the work of laymen, modern philosophy's point of departure was introspective, reflective, and man-centered. René Descartes (1596-1650), who desired philosophy to be as precise as mathematics, felt that man, prior to experience, had innate ideas which lead to the innate idea of God. His method evolved into philosophical rationalism, emphasizing mind over matter, sense experience, and focused its attention on laws of thought and the universal. Baruch Spinoza (1632-1677) attempted to formulate ethics according to geometrical demonstration. Prominent also in this period were Gottfried Leibnitz (1646-1716), co-inventor of calculus, and Immanuel Kant (1724-1804), who formulated the nebular hypothesis as an explanation of the world's origin. Kant concluded that devotion to all mankind was nothing less than a rational obligation. He felt that the duty to treat others as ends and never as means is as binding on the individual as the most conclusive formula of mathematics or physics. The Kantian ideal requires that man put aside all egotistic motives in favor of a response to the law as a rational duty. He conceived of man as less than man if he allows his decisions in life to be controlled by self-love. Yet, hardly has the admission of man's duty been made when the problem of performance emerges. While it is not particularly difficult to say how man should act, to take Kant's philosophy seriously is to assume that no man can be moral, since it is impossible for man to act solely and always out of rational duty.

Drawing from both rationalists and empiricists, Kant accepted intellectual knowledge as universal, like the rationalists, and insisted, like the empiricists, that all genuine knowledge can be drawn from experience. He did not believe that man is capable of knowing the essence of things; yet he held that scientific knowledge is possible without lapsing into skepticism and relativism.

A sharp reaction to rationalism was led by men who insisted on testing the validity of an idea by tracing the idea to the initial experience because each denied the ability of man to understand abstractions without objects. These empiricists included Thomas Hobbes (1588-1679), George Berkeley (1685-1753), and David Hume (1711-1771). Of this group, only Berkeley accepted innate ideas.

G. W. F. Hegel (1770-1831) viewed reality as the development of a rational principle, Mind, the totality of reality. In his *Phenomenology of Mind,* he emphasized the fact that everything must be seen as one or another phase of mind as it runs the course of history and that things are forever capable of further development and perfection.

Karl Marx (1818-1883) used some Hegelian methodology but insisted that matter, not mind, is what is developing in history. For Marx, the clash of the proletariat (thesis) and the bourgeoisie (antithesis) eventually give rise to a classless society (synthesis).

Other reactions to rationalistic tradition have been seen in both naturalism and pragmatism. Philosophical naturalism sees no meaning to any order but natural order. It negates any idea of interference by the supernatural. Both insist again on experience as the only source of meaning. Triggered by Darwin's "evolutionary breakthrough," leaders in the movement have included William James (1843-1910) and John Dewey (1859-1952).

The False Religion of Hopeless Humanism

If science can presumably assimilate a religious ideal built around the primacy of human values, humanism is that religion. In place of idle speculation about questions of providence and creation, the humanist is content to investigate problems of individual and social integration. Man is very much here; the duty of both religion and science is to find the causal connections which will prevent individuals from being frustrated either by the universe or by their relation to each other. Labor problems must be studied and solved. Satisfactory means for equitable processing and distribution of food and clothing must be discovered. Instead of belittling himself as a chronic sinner, man must begin to realize his potentialities for self-perfectibility, says the humanist. In opposition to all theories of universal predestination, determinism, or fatalism, humanism believes that human beings possess true freedom of creative action and are, within reasonable limits, the masters of their destiny.

Edward J. Carnell includes in *A Philosophy of the Christian Religion* (William B. Eerdmans, Publishers, p. 234), this observation from Corliss Lamont's *Humanism as a Philosophy:*

> Whatever it be called, humanism is the viewpoint that men have but one life to lead and should make the most of it in terms of creative work and happiness; that human happiness is its own justification and requires no sanction or support from the supernatural sources; that in any case the supernatural, usually conceived of in the form of heavenly gods or immortal heavens, does not exist; and that human beings, using their own intelligence and cooperating liberally with one another, can build an enduring citadel of peace and beauty upon this earth.

Quoting Lamont, Carnell says that humanism views itself as an ethics that is positive, a repudiation of ascetic otherworldliness in favor of a buoyant this-worldliness. It is against all defeatist systems which either postpone happiness to an after-existence or recommend acquiescence to social injustice in this existence. Humanism has claimed to sustain a delicate balance between devotion to science and devotion to man. Science supplies the method of knowing, and man supplies the values for which the humanists strive.

But science cannot demonstrate that man OUGHT to be devoted to all men, for moral imperatives cannot be processed by the scientific method. Rationality does not help, for a this-worldly self-love says that it is irrational to sacrifice for those who are unlovely. Carnell believes that the more one tries to live selflessly for others, the more conscious he becomes of the power of self-love within him. He points out that the great confessional literature in history has been penned by those who have become sensitive to this conflict in their experience. For Carnell, this is the point where the first pilings are driven for the bridge which must lead man to God, for if man is to conquer the defect in his nature and fulfill his obligations to the "categorical imperative," he must be given a power which is not his own, a power which comes from a source of morality beyond himself.

Carnell continues on page 261 of his book, *A Philosophy of the Christian Religion:*

> The more earnestly one embraces the ideal of humanism, the less he is persuaded that the second table of the law (Ten Commandments) can remain without anchorage in the first. The fact that the humanistic ideal contains a duty which man's nature cannot assimilate is a patent proof that the ideal points beyond itself. While correctly perceiving the rule of our obligation, humanism yet fails to solve the problem of how a man can overcome the pride of his own ego and live according to the rule. It is impossible for mind to overpower the sinful tendencies of the heart, since such tendencies are nonrational vitalities not subject to the mind.
>
> In Christian language, man needs grace. The moral dilemma does not prove the existence of God. But what is clear is that if there is no power beyond man to assist him in doing the right, he is betrayed into a state of moral

desperation. The individual will hate himself if he denies the right, and he will be uneasy with himself if he confesses it.

Humanism without God is like an engine without power, a sun without light, music without notes, and mathematics without numbers.

The Amazing Contradictions Inherent in Existentialism

In the nineteenth century, as a strong reaction to Hegelian philosophy, the existentialist movement arose. Leaders in the movement included Soren Kierkegaard (1813-1885), Artur Schopenhauer (1788-1860), Friedrich Nietzche (1844-1900), and others who believed that an element of the irrational is present in the world and especially in the actions of man. They emphasized *will* rather than *intellect* and called for a corresponding freedom, commitment, and engagement. The now living Jean-Paul Sartre (born 1905) insists on a dialectical development in the world, sometimes using Hegelian terminology; yet his emphasis on the irrational and the absurd and his rejection of the Absolute separate him from Hegel.

The existential movement is a religion of "feeling," rather than a religion of faith based on the historical fact of Jesus. The movement grew out of the abandonment of humanism, which since the Renaissance had represented the belief of the inherent goodness of man and the inevitability of his progress. Since these lofty assumptions have been somewhat shattered because of the shocking revelations of man's inhumanity to man in the twentieth century, the drift of Western culture has been away from romanticism and a naturalistic philosophy which has proved rather disillusioning.

Humanism, because of the shocking, brutal events of the twentieth century, was faced with the unpleasant implications of nihilism and despair. The only solution remaining seemed to be a non-rational one. What man's head could not do, his heart might do. His head says the world has no meaning, but his heart can create a meaning that he can accept. Thus, the existentialist is allowed to possess a logical absurdity without any stigma.

The kind of guilt man feels when he fails to treat all men as ends and never as means is described by Kierkegaard, who caricatures the ethicist as one who offers a full semester's course on the moral imperative but would not face the question whether he or any of his acquaintances is ethical in his person, since such judgment would be unethical.

So-called Christian existentialists, such as Niebuhr, Barth, Bultmann, and Brunner join Kierkegaard in the assumption that much of Christian tradition is based on the "non-fact." For instance, to them the historical fact of the resurrection of Christ is completely unimportant; it is the *idea* of resurrection or eternal life that is important. Describing their position in the "leap of faith" category, they indicate that the bigger the leap, the bigger the faith, which proposition assumes that Christianity has very little historic basis and that the "Christ figure" can represent what is ultimate goodness to any man. In his book, *The New Evangelicalism,* Ronald Nash affirms that these "leap of faith" thinkers have every right to formulate their own system of religion; what they do not have is the right to call it Christianity or attempt to tie it to historical Christianity.

While Kierkegaard chose theism as the best framework within which to express individualistic existentialism, Jean-Paul Sartre chose atheism. Sartre makes several attempts to form an intellectual refutation of God's existence, but finally rests his case on existential considerations. Since arguments against God's existence are existentially irrelevant, (even as arguments for his existence are), Sartre's magic lamp of freedom cancels God's existence just as Kierkegaard's magic lamp brought him into existence. Rejecting expressions of authority which might give the individual an excuse for not being the author of his own choices. Sartre affirms that man's basic state of mind when confronting reality is the realization that everything is "too much"—consequently *nausea*. To Sartre, death is an overpowering absurdity. The bitter contradiction is that while man has a duty to shape his own life and world around him, he is constantly threatened by death, which Sartre calls a "cancellation always possible of what I can be." He sees man in a hostile world, full of absurdities, void of any supernatural help:

"Man can count on no one but himself; he is alone, abandoned on earth in the midst of his infinite responsibilities, without help, with no other aim than the one he sets himself, with no other destiny than the one he forges for himself on this earth."

What abysmal despair!

The Full-orbed Glory of the Christian Faith

The Christian religion faithfully, fearlessly, frankly faces the problem of human sin. In almost every culture, anthropologists have noted some acknowledgment of sin or a guilty conscience and an almost universal feeling that the gods or God must be appeased by some sort of blood sacrifice. If, like the Greeks, man's gods are as capricious as those of the Olympic Council, the problem of an awesome, Holy God poses no real barrier. But if, as according to the Jewish concept, He is holy and cannot, in reality, look upon sin, then the fact of a substitutionary offering cannot be shrugged off. In the Old Testament, God made very definite and specific statements about acceptable worship; he indicated both the time, place, and conditions that he would meet with men. For the sin offering to be acceptable, to be adequate for the sins of the whole world, the coming one anticipated by all the prophets would, like the Passover Lamb, have to be without sin. Hence, by taking on the form of a man, God could, in Christ, offer himself for the sins of the world, reconcile his mercy and love with his justice, holiness, and righteousness, and become both the Just and the Justifier (Romans 5).

When Isaiah says in Chapter 53 that all have sinned—that each has turned to his *own* way, he verifies the idea that while every man does not turn the *same* way, every man turns away (from God). Turning away may involve murder (conceived in hatred), adultery (conceived in lust), idolatry (worshipping things), or unbelief (doubting God). The sin may even be, as James 4:17 indicates, to know to do good and to fail to do it. Whatever the case, the universality of sin is affirmed in the Scripture with such consistency that it seems almost impossible to ascertain where theologians find a doctrine for the inherent goodness of man apart from God. The implicit fact seems to be that man cannot please God until something is done about his human nature, until a radical change takes place. The message is not that a man goes to hell because of his sins, for all have sinned and fallen short of God's glory. The unforgivable sin is the unforgiven sin—the sin of rejecting God's way of escape, the sin substitute, Christ Jesus.

The heart of God is revealed as one who has "no pleasure in the death of the wicked," who is "not willing that any should perish, but that all should come to repentance," and whose final invitation to a part in his Kingdom is that "whosoever will may come." Whatever distortions of this picture men may have formulated should have been cleared in Jesus' parable of the prodigal son, which is, in effect, a picture of the father's heart—eager to receive and forgive and reinstate and bless, making the first step forward once the son had "come to himself." The whole question becomes an act of "imputed righteousness," not that man becomes righteous through a system of self-improvement, but that God's plan for man (who had failed in every effort to keep the commandments) could, by identifying with Christ's death and resurrection, receive the very Person of Christ, the indwelling Holy Spirit, who could accomplish for man both positionally (before God) and experientially (before men) what all attempts at rule-keeping had failed to do.

The crucifixion of Christ seems a travesty if any of the existing forms of religion or philosophy were sufficient. The misery of the cross, certainly the physical horror but more especially the travail of his soul and the agony of his separation from God, seems superfluous if any other prevailing religious system were adequate for man's need or if man's perfectibility precludes any need for divine intervention. If the Bible teaches anything consistently, it is that man inherited from Adam a sin nature, not that any man is as depraved as he could be, but rather that all men by nature, unless God intervenes, will inevitably make those choices which do not honor God and which reveal a rebellious attitude toward God, violating whichever of his laws are most appealing and most at hand to be violated. The sins will be different, as the personalities and occasions for sins differ. The sin is essentially the same: unbelief, or doubting God. When man is spoken of as being a sinner first by nature and later by choice, this does not indicate that every man is as vile as he can possibly be. Although marred by sin, he is still created in God's image and retains some lofty and idealistic characteristics of unfallen man. But a perfectly holy God demands that his people be like him; and when they fail, he offers them the righteousness of his Son as their imputed righteousness. Thus, even though we have sinned, are we gloriously, marvelously saved.

The Life of the Christian in This World, Waiting for the Coming of the Lord

Critics are often quick to point out the fallacy of the oblivion of the so-called Christian to the needs of this world and his absorption with "pie-in-the-sky-bye-and-bye." While the indictment is no doubt deserved in many cases, and while no student of history could deny the horrors as well as the absurdities that have been perpetrated in the name of God and the church, it is grossly unfair to judge the product by its counterfeits. Jesus promises his disciples abundant life. He admonishes his followers to be the salt of the earth (a preservative against corruption) and the light of the world (to illumine darkness). Hence, the Christian who fails to realize his obligations in *this* world is acting contrary to the clear and specific admonitions set forth in the Scripture. While his goals are sometimes the same as those of the humanist, two distinct differences are noticeable:

(1) The source of power to perform the "oughts" comes from the presence and power of the indwelling Christ.

(2) The foundation for his commitment is his vertical relationship with God which sets in motion a corresponding horizontal relationship with his fellow man.

In other words, to love God is to love what God loves. And God so loved the world that he gave His Son.

Old Testament writers stressed the concept that a God of love, justice, and holiness expects to see those qualities abound in his followers in *this* world. The prophets were not necessarily social reformers, although they were deeply concerned with the social and moral problems of their day. The real source of their social passion and effectiveness was their concern for the will of God, rather than the welfare of men. For them, what was good was what God required; what was evil was what he forbade or disapproved. They saw beyond external appearances to the real causes for social inequalities and injustices; they believed that men and nations needed above all else to be right in their relationships to God. They were convinced that if men understood the nature of God and were right in their relations with him, they would be right in their relations with one another. *Righteousness above ritual* was their constant plea.

Amos admonished his people, saying that the Lord hated their feasts, would not accept their offerings, and was not pleased with their music because of their injustice to their fellow man. He attacked with vigor the oppression of the poor, accompanied by self-indulgence and luxurious living; he demanded, from God's point of view, justice, equity, and honesty. Hosea foresaw God's judgment coming upon Israel because of man's sins against his fellow man. Isaiah characterized God as a God of holiness, justice, mercy, peace, and steadfast love, and called forth corresponding qualities from His followers. Micah summed up most of the ethical teachings of the prophets: humility of bearing and conduct, justice, and mercy. Zephaniah pronounced judgment from God upon Jerusalem for three sins: rebellion against God, inner defilement, and cruel or oppressive treatment of men. Habakkuk pronounced woes upon a man who heaps up what is not his own, gets evil gain for his house, builds a town with blood, founds a city on inequity, makes his neighbor drunk, or worships an idol.

All the prophets concurred that no man is acceptable to God unless he treats his fellow man fairly. In Psalm 15 the writer outlines the eleven requirements for "abiding in the presence of God," and it is interesting to note that none of these qualifications is ritualistic; rather, each is concerned with moral and ethical values stemming from a right heart attitude. The book of Proverbs is a gold mine of practical instruction for living in *this* world, with instructions for good physical, mental, and emotional health validated by physicians today.

The centrality of God and his expectations that his children should be like him are as evident in the life and teachings of Jesus as they are in the Old Testament. Again, the vertical-horizontal relationship is emphasized. When Christ was asked which is the greatest commandment, he replied, "You shall love the Lord your God with all your heart, and with all your soul, and with all your mind. And the second like it. You shall love your neighbor as yourself. On these two commandments hang all the law and the prophets." Since the commandments summarized the basic moral law, Christ indicated that if a man loved God, he would keep the first four of the Ten Commandments; if he loved man, he would keep the last six. He further expanded the term "neighbor" to make it as inclusive as human need when he admonished his followers to love their neighbors as themselves. William Barclay calls this the "Everest of all ethical teaching." Truly, a vigorous restatement of the historical Christian faith would restore the basis of our confidence in the power and presence of God and would lead our nation to health and vigor again. A return to the ethical teachings of Christ would reverse the rising curve of contemporary secularism and almost complete cynicism.

The apostles faithfully and fully carried out the letter and the spirit of the ethical mandates of the Lord, "teaching them to observe all things that I have commanded you." While emphasis in the New Testament is on the brevity of this life, as well as the imminent return of Christ, it is not Scripturally accurate to conclude that the result was intended to be, or did in fact result in a people "so heavenly minded that they were of no earthly good." In Acts 2 Luke writes that the early church "found favor with the people." He later records the fact that a comment even among the unbelievers about the early Christians was that they were the ones who had turned the world upside down.

The epistles of the New Testament present a picture of a people in intensest activity, motivated by the power of the Holy Spirit *within them* and by the promise of a returning Lord *to them.* Our lives are to be so fashioned today, not basing the hope of our souls on vain speculation, but upon the historical truth of Christ. Let us, therefore, work, teach, and pray until the glorious consummation of the age.

5
What Not to Do
Until Jesus Comes Back

Then shall the kingdom of heaven be likened unto ten virgins, which took their lamps, and went forth to meet the bridegroom. And five of them were wise, and five were foolish. Afterward came also the other virgins, saying, Lord, Lord, open to us. But he answered and said, Verily I say unto you, I know you not. Watch therefore, for ye know neither the day nor the hour wherein the Son of man cometh (Matthew 25:1-2, 11-13).

And that, knowing the time, that now it is high time to awake out of sleep: for now is our salvation nearer than when we believed. The night is far spent, the day is at hand: let us therefore cast off the works of darkness, and let us put on the armour of light (Romans 13:11-12).

Amid the proliferation of things which are imperative before the coming of the Lord, let us also discuss a proscribed listing. Some behavior, much thought, and a myriad of actions are clearly prohibited. Accentuation of positive duties and emphasis on proper attitudes ought not to obscure the negations of the gospel. Jeremiah was informed during his commissioning service that he had six mandates, two-thirds of which were negative. He was commissioned "to root out, and to pull down, and to destroy, and to throw down," and only then would he be able "to build and to plant." (Jeremiah 1:10). Paul recognized that the Christian message mixed rebuke and warning with grace and mercy in producing the grand scheme of the ages. He reflected that our intensely powerful weaponry from God was to be employed "to the pulling down of strong holds," and "the casting down of imaginations and every high thing that exalteth itself against the knowledge of God" (2 Corinthians 10:4-5).

The biblical passages before us are both proposals for successful last-day living and cautions about programs of life designed to end catastrophically. As I read the eschatological sayings of Jesus, I discover that the details of our Lord's program for the eschaton are less clearly delineated than is his prescription for preparedness. He was stringently absorbed in the subject of readiness for the coming of the Bridegroom. The recurring admonition is "watch." The calamity is to slumber or to sleep. The present tragedy is that the churches of our Lord often slumber, becoming lax in convictions and ministries. If we awaken, there are negatives—things we must not do. As often as not, these are subtle dangers frequently appearing under the guise of good while harboring the guile of Satan which immerses the believer and the church in the gall of bitterness. What are the dangers—these pitfalls to avoid?

The Pitfall of Religious Syncretism

During the raging polio epidemic of the late '40's and early '50's, a mother in a South Texas town rushed her eight-year-old boy to the hospital. Because of previous tragedies which had already ravaged that community, a premature diagnosis was made, and the child was vigorously treated for polio. Within hours he paled and died. Autopsy revealed an ailment with symptoms similar to those of polio, but with a nature altogether distinct. Had diagnosis been accurate, not the outer look, the child could have been saved. The obvious appearance, the outer look, the first feeling had been substituted for the real and the true.

This same condition can occur in Christianity. Efforts to synthesize the "best elements" in assorted views into one all-encompassing faith are varied and profuse. For example, the Bahai faith sought to extract the best from Islam, Buddhism, and Christianity, amalgamating them into a world faith. Transcendental Meditation has sought to capture the mind of Eastern spiritual contemplation and to make it palatable to Western tastes. Far more formidable and infinitely more subtle for the churches of our Lord has been the development of ecumenism. The ecumenical movement has asserted that the trouble with the church is her monetary, ideological, organizational, and theological diversification. The world wants to see a united front! The church is asked to minimize distinctives, accentuate common practices and teachings in order to entice the world to hear.

There are serious flaws in the rubric of ecumenism, and one of the things our churches ought not to do until Jesus comes is to become absorbed in ecumenism. Here are the reasons:

(1) The syncretistic whole inevitably is flavored predominantly by the majority view. For example, the majority of those entering the present organizational church unions cry out much about the social responsibilities of the church but have little to say about sin, the Savior, and salvation. What has been lost is the clear concept of a marvelous redemption based on an eternal plan of God. In any such movement, what is sacrificed is likely to be of greater value than that which is retained. Jesus emphasized that many are called, but few are chosen. When the disciples on one occasion attempted to force conformity of a disciple who did not follow them, Jesus clearly remonstrated with his own men. Jesus also cautioned that he had sheep who were not of the present fold. Ecumenism has a tendency to make us sacrifice the distinct doctrines that produce biblical and vital Christianity.

(2) Ecumenism fails to recognize that the universal church can never be assembled on earth. In essence, the ecumenical movement is no better than Thomas Munzer and the Zwickau prophets of the Reformation who attempted to bring in Christ's Kingdom without the Anointed One. When Jesus comes back there will be one church, one bride of Christ! Until then, we

have no other alternative but to maintain our distinctives.

(3) Ecumenism is heedless of the prophecies relating to a great religious establishment, universal in its scope, closely related to the state, oppressive and malignant, opulent and pompous, which will control the religious scene in the last days. Read the seventeenth chapter of the Revelation.

Organized ecumenism has suffered a temporary setback. A new and proliferating form has surfaced. Avoiding the difficulties inherent in organizational amalgamation, this new approach has capitalized on experience. Neopentecostalism or the charismatic movement hosts Roman Catholicism, Arminian Protestantism, and occasionally Calvinistic Protestantism, and even Mormonism, all under the broad umbrella of the "baptism of the Holy Spirit" as documented by the experience of glossolalia. Individual organizations are left intact, but all differences are unimportant if one has had the *experience* of tongues.

But experiential syncretism is no less dangerous than organizational syncretism. Both consider the objective doctrines of the faith expendable if only a certain prescribed goal can be obtained. If anything, organizational ecumenism is the nobler since its focus is theoretically not inward and emotional, but outward, committed to ministry and change. Until Jesus comes back, Bible-believing Christians ought not to be involved in religious syncretistic movements. The local church is the base of operation. Christ is the message. The field is the world!

The Morass of Religious Minutiae

Until Jesus comes back we must not become prodigious expounders of peripheral queries which engender confusion rather than confidence. Paul warned that in the last days men would be ever learning, yet somehow incapable of arriving at truth. He cautioned that foolish questions ought to be avoided, knowing that these only produce strife.

"But foolish and unlearned questions avoid, knowing that they do gender strifes" (2 Timothy 2:23).

"Ever learning, and never able to come to the knowledge of the truth" (2 Timothy 3:7).

In the last two decades the theological morticians have debated God's demise, and philosophers have philosophized about what is meaningful religious language and what is not. New Testament scholars still expend hours in efforts to determine who depended upon whom in the Synoptic Gospels.

The central doctrines of the Scriptures deserve our finest intellectual expertise and ought to be the focus of our evangelical persuasion. The logic of that position is inescapable and irrefutable. Imagine a man purporting to be a great heart surgeon. However, he is continually infatuated with his golf and tennis exploits and reads the sports news more avidly than the medical journals. His week-ends are devoted to yachting, and he is absorbed with his interest on Wall Street. Who wants to submit to his scalpel? If I must have delicate, life-sustaining cardiac surgery, give me a surgeon whose life and breath are the mastery of his art!

Until Jesus comes back we dare not debate peripheral issues too much. We must master our commission to diagnose the sin of the race and prescribe in the most communicatively successful way the remedy of Christ's blood as remission for sin.

Nor can we circumvent the ministry which God has given us. Social concerns and environmental improvements are worthy of the believer. Drives for the eradication of cancer, poverty, or illiteracy are certainly aspects of genuine Christian concern. But all of these may be fostered by a society which knows nothing of the grace of our Lord in salvation. The distinctive tasks of the church, and therefore, the ministries that ought to claim our major interests, are still evangelizing, baptizing, and teaching for Jesus!

The Defeat of Religious Pride

Until Jesus comes back we must not become overconfident and proud in our status and history. Western Christianity bathes itself in opulence which would astonish the believers of the first century. Churches today constantly engage in funding drives, but few experience financial limitations of permanent or painful consequence. We have both community acclaim and status and in too many respects we are like Laodicea—"rich, and increased with goods, having need of nothing." As such we are also in hourly peril of sailing along blissfully unaware of our spiritual wretchedness and poverty!

Status, financial success, popularity, numerical increase—these are not inherently evil. On the contrary, these blessings of God ought to serve as daily reminders of the sweet-smelling fragrance of the graciousness of our God. But we must never become dependent upon our historical success. We cannot stake the future on our affluence. Our organizational structure can become a hideous and dangerous monster, threatening to devour its constituency, rather than a domesticated beast of burden to serve the people. In short, we must remember until Jesus comes back that it is "not by might, nor by power, but by my Spirit, saith the Lord."

The Danger of Religious Regimentation

Until Jesus comes back we must not succumb to organizational constriction. Denominational boards, agencies, associations, and conventions can easily be moored to outdated strategy. All are susceptible to the deadly peace of the status quo. These structures may provide the framework for magnificent accomplishment, or they may become an albatross around the neck of God's people. The sterling movements of Christian history have often grown out of individual conviction and effort, not out of organized, ecclesiastical programs. Larger organizations must reflect progressive thinking and, above all, sensitivity to the nuances of the leadership of the Holy Spirit. Until Jesus comes back, organizational life must neither dominate nor constrict our purpose and goal.

Regimentation can occur at a local level also. A church may become a slave of the program she has spawned. The moment a congregation becomes program-centered rather than person-centered, people suffer and programs demonstrate that they are hardly benevolent dictators. Certainly we must have planning. Programs are vehicles for ministry. But when they become brittle, losing flexibility, bowing to no one, then the Spirit of the Lord is quenched. Until Jesus comes back we must minister to people in a people-centered program.

The Peril of Religious Isolationism

If religious regimentation is a significant problem, religious isolationism can be equally costly. Until Jesus comes back we cannot afford to sever legitimate ties of cooperation and fellowship. Although the religion of the Bible is an intensely individualistic faith, corporate expression of that personal relationship with God is one of the glorious themes of Scripture. The patriarchal family worshipped together with the patriarch as the priest. The *Qahal*, the congregation of Israel, dominates the entirety of the Old Testament from Exodus to the exile. The exile produced the synagogue, "the gathering together," and the Lord established His *ekklesia*, the "called-out fellowship." This fellowship of the Spirit is central in the history of early Christianity.

Cooperation with other churches of like faith—those who believe the Book and who trust the Savior—is essential to the edification of all. This includes denominational fellowships. Some meaningful areas of cooperation and fellowship will even transcend denominational lines. What we cannot afford is to withdraw ourselves from other believers. Until our Lord comes in heavenly splendor we must not isolate ourselves and think that we alone are left to stand for God.

Conclusion

There are many other things we ought not to do until Jesus comes. But after observing the ecclesiastical scene for nearly fifty years, I am persuaded that these are some of the more important dangers ever present with us. In one sense, what we do until Jesus comes back is more important than what we do not do. On the other hand, our ability to accomplish the crucial tasks which we must achieve before Shiloh comes depends on avoiding the pitfalls of our spiritual obstacle course. We have sought to name some of the weights that we need to lay aside, enabling us to endure in the race God has set before us. Having rid ourselves of these encumbrances, let us press on toward the prize of our high calling in Christ Jesus.

PART III

WAITING IN PATIENCE, AND MINISTERING IN LOVE

[WAIT]

"Let not your heart be troubled: ye believe in God, believe also in me.

"In my Father's house are many mansions; if it were not so, I would have told you. I go to prepare a place for you.

"And if I go and prepare a place for you, I will come again, and receive you unto myself: that where I am, there ye may be also."

John 14:1-3

"For the Lord himself shall descend from heaven with a shout, with the voice of the archangel, and with the trump of God: and the dead in Christ shall rise first: Then we which are alive and remain shall be caught up together with them in the clouds, to meet the Lord in the air: and so shall we ever be with the Lord. Wherefore comfort one another with these words."

1 Thessalonians 4:16-18

WHEN WE SEE CHRIST

Oft-times the day seems long, our trials hard to bear,
We're tempted to complain, to murmur and despair;
But Christ will soon appear to catch His bride away,
All tears forever over in God's eternal day.

It will be worth it all when we see Jesus,
Life's trials will seem so small when we see Christ;
One glimpse of his dear face, all sorrow will erase,
So bravely run the race till we see Christ.

Sometimes the sky looks dark with not a ray of light,
We're tossed and driven on, no human help in sight;
But there is one in heaven, who knows our deepest care,
Let Jesus solve your problems—just go to Him in prayer.

Life's day will soon be o'er, all storms forever past,
We'll cross the great divide to glory safe at last;
We'll share the joys of heaven—a harp, a home, a crown,
The tempter will be banished, we'll lay our burdens down.

It will be worth it all when we see Jesus,
Life's trials will seem so small when we see Christ;
One glimpse of His dear face, all sorrow will erase,
So bravely run the race till we see Christ.

ESTHER KERR RUTHOL (1909-1962)

1
Strengthened by the Great Expectation

For our conversation is in heaven; from whence also we look for the Saviour, the Lord Jesus Christ: Who shall change our vile body, that it may be fashioned like unto his glorious body, according to the working whereby he is able even to subdue all things unto himself. Therefore, my brethren dearly beloved and longed for, my joy and crown, so stand fast in the Lord, my dearly beloved. I beseech Euodias, and beseech Syntyche, that they be of the same mind in the Lord. And I intreat thee also, true yokefellow, help those women which laboured with me in the gospel, with Clement also, and with other my fellowlabourers, whose names are in the book of life. Rejoice in the Lord alway: and again I say, Rejoice (Philippians 3:20-4:4).

This chapter includes "The Great Expectation," because I could not find a more characteristic name for the attitude of the early Christian believers. They had a great, pervading, enduring hope. The early Christian church was motivated by a secret that is laid bare for us in the pages of the literature they left behind. How could such a little, feeble, unknown, almost infamous band face so staggering a task as the conversion of the Roman world? And yet they did it boldly, confidently, triumphantly, and victoriously. In a comparatively short while as human history goes, they transformed the whole empire.

Today you never see an idol-deity of Venus (the Roman goddess of love and beauty). You never see people worshipping Dionysius (the Greek god of wine) or Demeter (the wife of Zeus and the supposed founder of the Eleusinian mysteries). You never see anyone serving in a temple of Jupiter (the chief of the gods) or of Mars (the god of war). Today you never see a worshipper at an oracle like the famous Oracle at Delphi. Yet, in the early days of the church that was the state religion of the civilized world. Anyone who did not bow down before the gods of the empire was looked upon as an enemy of the emperor and usually paid for his refusal to worship with his life. Nevertheless these Christians, so few and so feeble in themselves, faced the arenas of amphitheaters with their lions, the Roman soldiers with their crosses, and those cruel and terrible dungeons boldly, in confidence, and finally in triumphant victory.

What is the secret of that glorious victory? I do not see it in our churches today. Our mission work on some foreign fields may have continued for 100, 150, or 200 years, but in five years a Communist army can sweep down and wipe it all away. What is then left is a vestigial remnant. What we could not do in 200 years, a Communist army can do almost overnight. What was the secret of that unusual and holy energy that so moved and motivated those early Christians that they could turn the world rightside up?

The secret is found in their great expectancy. You show me what you hope for, what you work for, what you dream of, what you look forward to, and I can delineate exactly the character and nature of your life. Those early Christian churches were moved and motivated by a tremendous expectation which was this: "from whence . . . we look for the Saviour, the Lord Jesus Christ," descending in chariots of glory from the blue of heaven's skies. They looked for it, they waited for it, they believed in it, they gave themselves to it, and when they greeted one another or when they bade one another farewell, they said, *"Maranatha"* (the Lord is coming) or *"achri hou elthei,"* (till he comes). They never forgot his coming.

They were like the servants the Lord spoke of in Matthew

24. Their task was to watch and to wait. If two of them went on a trip together, as the shores of home faded away, they looked forward across the distant sea to the time when on the other side they would see their Lord. If one of them moved out of a house into another one, the new house was doubly sacred, because in those rooms they lived nearer to Jesus than they did in the old house they had left behind. If two of them separated and bade each other goodby, they did it in the fond hope that they would meet again in the nearer presence of the Lord. It permeated all of their lives; it colored everything they said. You find written large on the pages of the Holy Book this great expectancy that our Lord is coming again. "For our commonwealth is in heaven, from whence also we look for the Saviour, the Lord Jesus Christ."

They were not looking for a judge or a destroyer but for their Savior, their great and holy Deliverer. The eye of faith could see the heavens rolled back like a scroll, and the ear of faith could hear his chariot wheels descending from the sky with the legions of angels, tier upon tier, coming with their Lord in glory.

Modern Loss of Expectancy

Our modern church has so largely forsaken that hope. It has grown weary in watching, and the passing centuries have clouded that vision and have shut it away from most of the hearts of God's people. For one thing, ridiculous fanatics have almost turned us away from even thinking of it. False prophets have arisen and said, "Lo, here!" And other false prophets have arisen and said, "Lo, there!" And other false followers have set times and seasons, and the hope has sometimes become nebulous and empty.

Often in these days there arise men who purport to understand the deep secrets of the Bible. They will identify a man like Mussolini as the one who is recreating the Roman Empire. They will present him as the great Man of Sin (the Antichrist) who is to be revealed at the last time. I listened to that identification for years. And when it comes to nothing, those who have listened arrive at the conclusion that such a prophecy is pure fantasy. They decide there is no truth—there is no reality in prophecy at all. There is no actual return of Christ to be expected. They think we live in this world in a half-faith. They think that what might have happened back there as recorded in the Gospels could have been true, but there is no certain destiny, and there is not any future such as these martyrs who died in the faith believed in. Ah, my brother, I know there is a weird fanatical fringe that always attends the preaching of the gospel of the Son of God, but gospel truth and its great revelations, when properly interpreted, will never fall to the ground. The Lord has said it. It shall be. The Lord has spoken it. It shall come to pass. Our conversation, our citizenship, our commonwealth is in heaven. From thence we expect the Savior, the Lord Jesus Christ.

Our Lord came the first time after a long, long delay. Many scholarly men who write commentaries on the book of Genesis think that, when Eve was given her first son, Cain, and said, "I have gotten a man from the Lord," she thought Cain was the promised seed, the Deliverer that was to come from God. When Cain turned out to be a murderer with blood on his hands, what a great disappointment it was to our first mother! Yet the promise did not fall to the ground. How long ago Eve lived no man knows for certain. Though it was thousands and thousands of years in the past, she expected the Messiah in her day and time. He delayed, but he finally came. Our Lord Jesus Christ, the seed of the woman who would bruise the serpent's head, did come.

It is so, and no less certain with the other half of the Christian faith. Jesus said, "I am coming back again." The apostles reiterated that cry, "He comes! He comes!" Some day in the providence of God, at a time known only to him, he will keep his word, he will keep his promise, and we shall see our Savior descending from the sky.

We have now a Christianity and a faith that is half fulfilled. We have a beautiful story of redemption. We have a glorious message of salvation. We have a marvelous revelation of the beginnings of the Christian faith, as the Holy Spirit guided those first apostles and witnesses and evangelists. But is this all? Is man's death the end? Does all of our faith sink finally into the darkness of the abyss? Or is there a hope, is there a life, is there a light, is there a Lord beyond the grave? And is he coming again in triumph and in glory? All of these centuries that have passed, the Bible would say, are but the preparatory years for the glorious age that is yet to come. These centuries that have gone by are but the preludes, they are but the harbingers and the preparations for the marvelous, incomparable consummation that God has in store for his people. And that consummation occurs when the Lord comes, when he descends on clouds of glory with his saints and with his holy angels, when we shall see our Savior, the Lord Jesus Christ.

Human history to some people is like a great flat plain, and on that plain, humanity endlessly, purposelessly, blindly mills around and comes back finally to the ashes of the dead fires where they slept in the years gone before. But to us, history is a golden stairway. We pray, we struggle, we hope—then we lift up our faces to behold an open door into heaven, and at the head of a Jacob's ladder is the great consummating kingdom that is ours, promised for some glorious and triumphant day. "For our citizenship is in heaven, from whence also we look for the Saviour, the Lord Jesus Christ."

Assurance of Resurrection

According to Paul's inspired explanation of the coming of the Lord, his letter to the believers in Philippi presents some definite things that follow in view of the marvelous appearing of our Savior. The first one he mentions is this: "He shall change our vile body, that it may be fashioned like unto his glorious body, according to the working whereby he is able even to subdue all things unto himself." Christ Jesus will change us when he comes. We shall all be changed! The first thing that shall come to pass when our Lord descends in clouds of glory is this: God's saints will all be changed, in a moment, in the twinkling of an eye, at the last trump. These who have fallen asleep in Christ will be raised incorruptible, and we who are alive at his coming shall all be immortalized. We shall be given heavenly, glorified bodies (cf. 1 Corinthians 15:50-55).

Actually, the term *soma tes tapeinoseos* refers to our body of humiliation. Whoever translated that in 1611 as "this vile body" evidently had a touch of the Stoic contempt for the body, but there is no such thing as that in the Word of God. Greek philosophy taught that the body was contemptible and vile, that the seat of all sin and iniquity was in the body, that it was worthless, and that only *nous* (mind) or *psuche* (soul) was to be exalted and honored. The Bible and the Christian faith teach the direct opposite of that. The Christian doctrine is that this body is a house, it is a temple, it is the home of the soul, and it is to be resurrected and raised incorruptible and immortal, like the body of the Lord Jesus Christ.

That is why I have always felt that the burning of the body, though perfectly in keeping with Christian philosophy, should not be a part of our Christian practice. I could not conceive of the body of our Lord being cremated, but I can easily conceive of the body of our Lord being carefully wrapped and embalmed with spices, laid gently and lovingly in a tomb, and there sealed, awaiting the promised day of resurrection. I do not say that cremation of a body is ultimately wrong. The actual, final disposal of the dead is no different for ashes burned in a furnace, or for a physical frame turning to dust in the heart of the earth. Yet, those early Christians, who lived in a world of cremation, never cremated the body. That is the explanation for the origin of the catacombs. Denied the right to bury their loved ones, they dug down into the heart of the earth, and there in secret and subterranean passageways they lovingly laid their dead away. They believed in the resurrection of the dead. They believed in God's holy care of this house, the home of the soul. They looked forward to that time when God would change us in a moment, in the twinkling of an eye, gathering that precious dust out of the heart of the earth and refashioning it according to the likeness of the glorious body of our Lord Jesus Christ.

Archbishop Richard Whately of England (1787-1863) was lying on a bed of severe affliction, and finally of death. One of his chaplains, while trying to comfort him, happened to read Philippians 3:21. The Archbishop said to him, "Wait, say those words again." And he read again, ". . . change our vile body." Then the Archbishop said: "No! Read Paul's words. What did he say?" So the chaplain read it as Paul wrote it, ". . . who shall change our body of humiliation." This body, now subject to pain, age, disease, and death is a body of humiliation, but some day it shall be a glorious body. The Archbishop said to his chaplain: "Now you have it right. That is what he said, for God never made anything vile."

God shall change this body that now is in the valley of humiliation, bent and aged, and finally diseased and dying. He will fashion it anew like unto his own body of glory. But how? Paul describes the process as being accomplished according to the energy of God's ableness. Is not that a magnificent way to say it? "Fashioned . . . according to the working whereby he is able," according to the energy of his ableness. How does God take dust from the ground or out of the depths of the sea and resurrect the dead? He who created those stars and flung them into space, and he who gave us a body in the first place, that same infinite, mighty God is able, out of the dust of the ground, to raise up those who have fallen prey to the pale horseman of death, "according to the working whereby he is able even to subdue all things unto himself."

Our Life Till He Comes

Our great expectation not only points toward the future resurrection, but it clearly implies a new quality of life here and now. As Paul expresses it: "Therefore, my brethren dearly beloved and longed for, my joy and crown, so stand fast in the Lord, my dearly beloved." Stand fast in the Lord!

What a change in this man, Saul of Tarsus! Only a few years earlier Paul would have looked upon these Philippians as Gentile dogs, as blaspheming, uncircumcised heathen; yet now he writes to them as "my brethren, dearly beloved and longed for, my joy and crown . . . my dearly beloved." Notice how he heaps words of affection upon them—my twice-loved, my desired ones, my brethren. In view of this great hope of the coming of Christ, we as fellow members of the family of God are to stand fast in the Lord. Like a bird buoyed up by the air, like a fish in a sea in which it can live, so we in the promise of our coming Lord are to find strength for our lives.

A further implication, emphasized by Paul in this exhortation, is that in view of this great, holy expectation, we are not to be drawn into personal and futile altercation. "I beseech Euodias" (her name means literally "a prosperous journey") "and beseech Syntyche" (literally meaning "good fortune"), "that they be of the same mind in the Lord." In light of this great and stupendous revelation of the Lord, how can we be little and conniving, small and censorious, or full of furor, bickering, and backbiting? No, in view of this great hope we are to be together in the Lord.

Then Paul further writes, "Rejoice in the Lord alway: and again I say, rejoice." Look at the man writing that. Did anyone ever go through such trials as Paul? He was shipwrecked, beaten, stoned and left for dead, and many times imprisoned (see 2 Corinthians 11:23-29). Paul's Philippian letter comes from a

Roman prison. Yet, he writes, "Rejoice in the Lord alway." Not just at Christmas or Easter; but rejoice today, tonight, in the morning, tomorrow, all the time. Rejoice in the Lord. In prison, in suffering, in illness or in health, rejoice in the Lord.

We are not to rejoice in our temporal prosperity, or in our place in this world, or in anything the world has to give. I read one time of a king who was miserable. One of his sages said to him, "In order to be happy, wear the shirt of the happiest man in your realm." So he sent out all of his counselors and advisors to find the happiest man in the realm. They were ordered to bring him that man's shirt to wear. When the counselors came back they said: "O king, we have found the happiest man in the realm. But he does not have a shirt!" We are to be like that man. Any time we identify happiness and gladness and rejoicing with physical prosperity, with things in this life, we have turned God's whole equation around. Rejoice in the Lord, not in the abundance of things.

We are not even to be glad of our successes. When the seventy came back to Jesus and rejoiced saying, "Even the devils (demons) are subject unto us," Jesus said, "Rejoice not that the spirits are subject unto you; but rather rejoice, because your names are written in heaven," in the Lamb's book of life (cf. Luke 10:17-20, Revelation 21:27). In view of our great, holy expectation, be glad and rejoice in Him.

Finally, Paul writes: "Let your moderation (*epieikēs*, literally "gentle" or "kind," thus a good translation would be your "forbearing spirit" or your "forbearance") be known unto all men. The Lord is at hand." In 2 Corinthians 10:1 Paul uses a form of this same word, *epieikeias*, to speak of the gentleness of Jesus, the forbearance of Jesus. What does he mean by the word here? The Lord is at hand, our Savior is coming, therefore "let your forbearance be known unto all men."

What he means is simply this: we ought not to fret, we ought not to be downcast, and we ought never to be discouraged. We should never be in despair, "for our Lord is at hand." We are not to worry ourselves because of evildoers even if the whole world is covered with sin as in the antediluvian age, and there is only one righteous family in the earth. We are never to be discouraged. Look up, look up, the Lord is at hand! Nor are we to be discouraged by any of the vicissitudes and turns of life. "Why art thou cast down, O my soul? And why art thou disquieted within me?" And the Psalmist answered, "Hope thou in God" (Psalm 42:5, 11).

Does the fig tree refuse to blossom? Does the worm eat the root of the vine? Does the vine itself perish and dry and wither away? Does the day turn into night and the night into darkness and the darkness into a seven-fold horror more terrible than the night of Egypt? Does it? We are not to be discouraged. We are not to be cast down. The Lord is at hand! Look up! Up there in heaven is our ultimate and certain and final victory. "Let your forbearance be known unto all men. The Lord is at hand."

Someone asked, "Pastor, how does one get to be that way?" Let us find our answer in our Lord Jesus. The forbearance, the gentleness of Jesus is described like this: "He shall not cry, nor lift up, nor cause his voice to be heard in the street. A bruised reed shall he not break, and the smoking flax shall he not quench" (Isaiah 42:2-3; Matthew 12:19-20). What does it mean? It means simply that Jesus waited on God. He trusted and depended upon his Father. He was not upset and full of disquietude. In the storms that raged, he would lie asleep on a pillow in the boat. When others around were frightened and filled with agony and terror, he was quiet and confident in God. What a way to live, what a faith, what a hope!

"Let your forbearance be known unto all men. The Lord is at hand." We are not going to lose because he lives. We are not to be discouraged, for our Lord sees. We are not to be cast down; our Lord cares. We are not to think we have been forgotten; he watches over his own. Triumph and victory are ours. The Lord is at hand. "For our commonwealth is in heaven;

from whence also we look for the Saviour, the Lord Jesus Christ." The Lord's people are blessed in God, and the fullness of all the promises are ours, and we are his. Oh, that God would give us a precious hope that really lives in our hearts like the secret that moved those first devout Christians, who could face death, yet sing a song, who could be burned at the stake, yet rejoice in God their Savior, who could rot in a prison, yet never lose hope. Ah, the blessedness of such a faith, and of such a commitment of heart and life to the Jesus who is coming again!

2
Watching While We Work

For the grace of God that bringeth salvation hath appeared to all men,
Teaching us that, denying ungodliness and worldly lusts, we should live soberly, righteously and godly, in this present world;
Looking for that blessed hope, and the glorious appearing of the great God and our Saviour Jesus Christ;
Who gave himself for us, that he might redeem us from all iniquity, and purify unto himself a peculiar people, zealous of good works (Titus 2:11-14).

Herein is our love made perfect, that we may have boldness in the day of judgment: because as he is, so are we in this world (1 John 4:17).

The Asian metropolis of Sardis of Lydia, famous for its wealth and wisdom, was the stronghold of the wealthy despot, Croesus, and of the great Greek philosopher, Thales. However, neither wealth nor wisdom provide ultimate insurance. Indeed, they may very well lull one into catastrophic stupor. This is precisely the sad story of Sardis, the proud city that twice forgot to watch.

Considered impregnable in its construction on the slopes of Mount Tmolus, at the base of which ran the gold-bearing Pactolus River, Sardis stood poised for the invasion of Cyrus of Persia. Cyrus understood the magnitude of the task and offered enormous rewards to the man who found a way in. Hyeroeades, a Mardian soldier, observed a Lydian soldier as he deftly retrieved a fallen helmet. That evening Hyeroeades and a group of men slipped stealthily up the same approach, and to their astonishment found the city overconfident and unguarded. The fall of Sardis was thorough and rapid. In her self-confident drowsiness, she even repeated the same mistake a second time in later history.

One of our Lord's warnings to Sardis was "to watch," and "strengthen the things which remain." Our blessed Lord is continually calling his church to watchfulness. Again in the book of Titus the Spirit of our Lord directs Paul to inscribe an admonition to look or to watch for our Lord's return.

The Titus passage above brings together the appearances of our Lord. The grace of God became apparent in Jesus. The lucidity of the heavenly Father's eleemosynary act was inescapable for those who beheld the Saviour. The grace of God was experiential. Men could actually know Jesus and experience transformation of life as a result. However, the grace of God which came in Jesus was not merely quantitative, that is, salvation for eternity. Our Lord also endowed us with a qualitative life through the initial teaching ministry of our Lord, augmented by a continued instructional pedagogy of the Holy Spirit from within. Jesus taught us how to live until he comes back.

The Denying Part of the Watchful Christian

Jesus challenged his followers to "deny themselves." Living in the last days, watching for our Lord, involves the disciple in two essential denials.

(1) Ungodliness—The word *asebeian*, "ungodliness," is a term employed in the secular Greek of antiquity to describe deliberate disloyalty to the emperor. Herodotus uses the word to indicate an act of sacrilege. In other words, ungodliness is not only the absence of God in one's life and thought, but also the active rejection of God and the perpetuity of generally impious behavior. "Watching" for the Lord includes a posture of submission

and acquiescence to the Holy Spirit. A believer cannot decide for himself. He is committed to searching for the sovereign pleasure of the Creator. He is constrained to deny all ungodliness in his life or thought.

(2) Worldly Lusts—Examining the fruits of the pursuit of worldly-oriented pleasures and possessions ought to constitute a sufficient refutation of their values. But there is something about man's fallen nature that produces greed and excessive desire in us all. The word "lust" in this text is as vivid as it is terrifying. *Epithumias* is derived from *thumos* meaning "heat," and the proposition *epi* meaning "upon." Literally it means "heat upon heat" and thus "determination." Paul cautions against a worldly determination. Several reasons may be given for this.

Worldly determination is based wholly on the limited understanding of tainted man. The wisdom and the mind of the Spirit are not consulted. Believers are often happy for Jesus to be our advocate as long as that implies "defender," but they are reluctant if advocate means "counselor." The Christian is one committed to discerning the mind of the Lord, crucifying self so that Jesus may live through him. Not our world desires, but his heavenly will must govern our thoughts and actions.

Worldly determination is persuasion based on the apprehension and attainment of *kosmikos*, "worldly ends," and not *ouranios*, "heavenly consequences." The worldly is by definition temporal, ephemeral, transitory, limited. By contrast the heavenly is eternal, immutable, of enduring value. Our minds ought to be stayed upon heavenly things until Jesus comes back. Denial, refusal, abandonment of ungodliness and worldly lusts constitute the continuing walk of faith.

The Affirming Part of the Christian Faith

Paul is concerned with denials, but he has not omitted the affirmations of positive Christian behavior. This passage provides us with an internal command which will inevitably result in a certain kind of external behavior involving both horizontal and vertical relationships.

(1) Soberly—The initial relationship of life is with one's self. Paul calls for sobriety, but the intent far exceeds abstinence from drink. In fact, this word *sophronos,* "soberly," has a wealth of etymological history. In general it means "rational," but the various shades of rationality include freedom from illusion, intellectual soundness, purposefulness, discretion. Euripides even used it to mean modesty and decorum. The present age demands of the believer an intellectual perspicuity, a freedom from that which is not real, a sense of purpose, goal, and destiny, and a certain modesty and discretion characteristic of those who know that salvation is not of their own making.

John Bunyan, preaching from Bedford jail, making lace for his blind daughter to sell, exercised this sobriety. His sense of who he was in relation to God and his awareness of a divine mission sustained him through those dark, incomprehensible hours. Until Jesus comes back, the believer ought to be free of excesses, sober for the Lord.

(2) Righteously—"Righteously" has reference to our horizontal relationships to other men. Because we love God with all of our hearts, attitudes toward the whole of God's creation are softened. Righteous living is not mandatory for believers for the purpose of attaining a just standing before God. However, righteous living, the absence of any act of unnecessary advantage over a brother, is required as a result of our justification through God's mercy. Faith without works is confessing faith but not possessing faith and, hence, is really no faith at all. An experience with Christ will alter our reactions to men and color our behavior with love.

(3) Godly—Not only must the believer maintain inner sobriety and outward righteousness, but also he must demonstrate upward godliness. *Eusebos* or "godly" has reference to a life which features a tone of reverence for God and piety of walk growing out of that reverence. Though no acceptable degree of sobriety

or righteousness can ever be achieved without a proper vertical relationship to God, a diluted measure of the former requisites may be attained. But this last term implies that all of life is governed by a keen awareness of the presence of the Lord in the life of the believer. This cannot be imitated.

The Looking and Expectant Waiting
Part of the Christian Life

Jesus emphasized the necessity of watching. Five distinct times it is recorded that Jesus taught an attitude of watchfulness for his return. Part of what it means to be looking for the Lord's return has been delineated above. To look for his return is to conform to a program of prescribed discipleship, to follow him, to live Jesus' kind of life. Additionally, there is an attitude, an expectancy, an anticipatory spirit which ought to characterize us until Jesus comes back. This is "looking for that blessed hope"!

"Looking" is a translation of *prosdechomai,* a word of keenest anticipatory content. The word is used by Josephus to indicate the eager anticipation of certain Jews for the hope of their salvation. Interestingly, the same word is chosen by New Testament writers to project the eager anticipation of Simeon, the aged saint of Jerusalem who "waited for the consolation of Israel," and of Joseph of Arimathea who was "waiting for the Kingdom of God." "Looking" means an active, positive, eager hope.

The blessed hope is not an *event* in isolation but a *person* who fills the event of his return with significance. The whole event of a former prisoner from the war in Asia disembarking from the plane and stepping forward to greet his family from which he has been estranged for years is dramatic and profound. Excitement and pathos pour through the veins of participants and spectators as well. But the depths of meaning and significance are plumbed only by the lonely soldier and the grateful family reunited in a moment of ecstasy. However moving the circumstances, it is the *person* who gives greatest meaning to the event.

The same is true of our Lord's glorious return. The immaculate splendor of the heavenly spectacle will dazzle our eyes and excite our emotions. The heavenly choir will charm our ears with divine resonance, and the saints of the ages will delight us with their praise. What an experience it will be to join the four and twenty elders in casting our victor's crowns before the Lamb! But it is the *Lamb* that makes the difference. The revelation of Jesus provides meaning for the whole.

Three major descriptive terms were employed by the authors of our New Testament to picture the Lord's return. *Apokalupsis* emphasized the unveiling of that which had been at least partly hidden. Now we walk by faith, but when Jesus comes, the King is unveiled and we walk in celestial realms by sight.

Parousia is indicative of actual presence. Our Lord is coming to be with us. He has been with us all the time. He promised this presence in the Great Commission and fulfilled it in the abiding ministry of the Holy Spirit. But we are destined for a more profound encounter with the imminent One. Emmanuel will come again in his glorified body to make his presence visibly known.

In our passage from Titus the word for the "appearing" of Christ is *epiphaneian.* Translations of the term might be "appear," "give light," or "shine." The idea seems to be that our Lord will come with radiant splendor suggestive of his exalted position. The word also suggests suddenness. The appearing of our Lord will be a surprise to many. But until Jesus comes we ought to be watching for his return.

Now note how our Lord is identified. The coming One is the Great God and our Savior Jesus Christ. Can there be any question that Paul conceived Jesus to be wholly God as well as fully man? Did not the councils of Nicea and Chalcedon properly evaluate the New Testament data in affirming Christ's unmitigated humanity and undiluted deity? The Savior is God!

Jesus is God!

Notice that the appearance of this Savior God is called the blessed hope. "Blessed" indicates "happiness," "a preferred state or condition," or "fortunate." Why is the hope of God's people called "blessed?"

(1) The coming of our Lord marks the blessed end to the labor of the Lord's church. Taken up to be with the Lord in the air, the saints will enter into the rest of God. No more strife, no longer the threat of death, no invasion of sorrow and remorse, no plague of pain! All things will have become new.

(2) The hope is blessed because it inaugurates the last era of the redemptive act of God in Christ. Tribulation and Kingdom Age are eclipsed ultimately by the dawning of the eternal order. The divine plan of reconciliation formed in the mind of God in the dim recesses of pre-cosmic eternity is ushered into its glorious consummation.

(3) The appearing of our Lord Christ spells the beginning of the end for our arch-enemy Satan and the kingdom of rebellion which has been his concoction. "Blessed" describes graphically the condition of the triumph of good over evil, Christ over Satan.

Finally, looking for Jesus is to watch for the "blessed hope." Hope is highly tentative in the English language. In saying "we hope to win the game," we mean that the outcome is probably much undecided and in doubt. But the use of hope in the New Testament is not contingent. Hope is unrealized but nonetheless certain. It is an unrealized certainty because God's promise is the same as an irrefutable oath. It cannot be broken. The hope for the return of Christ is to pine for that event of intervention with perfect knowledge that our Lord draws nearer every day.

All of the above is involved in "looking for" and "waiting for" the Lord. Until Jesus comes back, the church must live soberly, righteously, and godly, looking for the Lord!

3
Terror and Tenderness
in the Coming of Christ

If any man love not the Lord Jesus Christ, let him be Anathema Maranatha (1 Corinthians 16:22).

Paul wrote his epistles through an amanuensis. Perhaps Sosthenes who is mentioned in 1 Corinthians 1:1 is the amanuensis for that letter. Paul dictated all of his letters, but he had a habit that he always followed when he came to the end. He picked up the pen himself and wrote a concluding salutation. In the last verses of the second Thessalonian letter, Paul writes: "The salutation of Paul with mine own hand, which is the token in every epistle: so I write. The grace of our Lord Jesus Christ be with you all. Amen." The salutation of Paul with his own hand is the token of genuineness in every epistle. When he finished dictating he picked up the pen and wrote in his own hand a concluding word.

In the last chapter of the Galatian letter in the King James Version, verse 11 is translated like this: "Ye see how large a letter I have written unto you with mine own hand" (Galatians 6:11). What Paul actually said there was this: "You see with what large letters I write unto you with mine own hand." In that eleventh verse he picked up the pen himself and wrote like a beginner. Many New Testament theologians think there was something wrong with Paul's eyes, and thus when he wrote, he used great, big, box letters like a first grade schoolboy.

That same pattern is followed in the concluding remarks of the first Corinthian letter. Paul picks up the pen and writes:

"The salutation of me Paul with mine own hand. If any man love not the Lord Jesus Christ, let him be Anathema Maranatha. The grace of our Lord Jesus Christ be with you. My love be with you all in Christ Jesus. Amen." (1 Corinthians 16:21-24).

Do you notice those two unusual, untranslated words? *Anathema Maranatha.* They belong to the vernacular of Palestine in the day when Paul lived. One of them, *Maranatha,* is Aramaic. You find untranslated Aramaic words all through the New Testament. When Jesus healed the deaf man (Mark 7:34) he said, *"Ephphatha,"* that is, "Be opened." In Acts 1:19 the field is called *"Aceldama,"* that is, "the field of blood." *"Eli, Eli, lama sabachthani?"* is Aramaic for "My God, my God, why hast thou forsaken me?" (Matthew 27:46). One reason you will find those untranslated words in the Scriptures is that Aramaic is the language Jesus spoke, and it is the language that Paul used when he studied in Jerusalem.

In this Corinthian letter Paul employs one of those Aramaic words, *Maranatha.* But *Anathema* is a common Greek word. By some peculiar turn of fortune on the part of the translators it was also left untranslated, but the two words have nothing to do with one another as such; that is, *"Anathema Maranatha"* is not a phrase together. However, the way Paul uses them here does have a tremendous import that we need to recognize.

The Two Pillars of the Faith

What does *Anathema* refer to? Taken into our language literally, it is a plain, simple English word meaning "cursed." Originally the word meant "devoted completely," and thus came to refer to a thing that was devoted completely by God for destruction. For example, all of Jericho was devoted for destruction—it was accursed, and as such, all of it was to be completely destroyed (Joshua 6:17). The ancient cities of Sodom and Gomorrah were completely devoted for destruction. They were accursed, damned, finally and irrevocably rejected by God (Genesis 19:13). *Anathema* means a final, irremediable, irrevocable, eternal damnation. It is an awesome thing to say, "If any man love not the Lord Jesus Christ," he is accursed, he is damned, he is eternally devoted to destruction. Hell and damnation await him.

The word *Maranatha* is made up of two Aramaic words. *Marana* means "the Lord," and *tha* means "he comes"—thus *Maranatha* means "the Lord comes." Evidently in those early, primitive days the Jewish Christians would greet each other with the Aramaic word *Maranatha,* just like the Christians who were Greeks would meet one another with the Greek words, *achri hou elthei,* "till he come."

You see, there are two great pillars upon which the testimony of the gospel of Jesus Christ rests. One of those pillars is this: that Christ has come a first time and that he died for our sins. The other one is that being raised, he is coming again apart from sin in triumph. Those are the two great pillars of the Christian faith: in memory, the cradle and the cross; in hope, the conquest and the crown. He is coming again with tremendous power in clouds of glory with the saints and with all the holy angels of heaven. Between those two great doctrines like a bridge the fragile present hangs suspended. The tragic thing is that we have come to the day when men have lost faith in the atoning cross of the Son of God, and they have lost any expectancy for the day when he will gloriously come again. However the modern faith is and however the churches of our modern life may be, the testimony of the Bible and the faith of the early Christians was, first, that the Lord Jesus had come to die for our sins and, second, that the Lord Jesus is coming again in glory and triumph to purge the world of all wrong and unrighteousness.

The Two-fold Response to the Coming of Christ

Now look how that final salutation in 1 Corinthians is put together. It stands as a very plain illustration of the whole fabric of the gospel of Christ. One part is terror and the other part is tenderness, and they are right there together. Look at it. "The salutation of me Paul with mine own hand. If any man love not the Lord [if any man spurns the overtures of love and mercy, the grace of Jesus Christ], let him be *Anathema.*" That is not a wish; it is a prophetic warning. If any man turns from Christ, damnation awaits him; the torment of fire and destruction awaits him. Then immediately, in the next breath, in the next syllable, there it is: "*Maranatha* [he is coming] The grace of our Lord Jesus Christ be with you. My love be with you all in Christ Jesus. Amen." Just like that!

The terror and the tenderness of the gospel message of Jesus is seen all the way through the New Testament. When a man preaches just about heaven and just about the atoning work of Christ and just about the sweet things of the Christian gospel—if he preaches only that—he is in no wise declaring the whole counsel of God. When a man preaches the whole gospel of Christ, he will find that there are things in the Book that make one's soul tremble. Horrible things, terrible things, things of hell, destruction, and damnation are in that Book. But always in the New Testament message, right after the damnation, in the next verse and in the next syllable, there will be the pouring out of the compassionate heart of God. The sweet pleadings of the Holy Spirit bring you to tears. There they are in the Book, right side by side. That is the gospel message. Look at it here in 2 Thessalonians 1:7-10 as Paul says:

> "And to you who are troubled rest with us, when the Lord Jesus shall be revealed from heaven with his mighty angels, In flaming fire taking vengeance on them that know not God, and that obey not the gospel of our Lord Jesus Christ: Who shall be punished with everlasting destruction from the presence of the Lord, and from the glory of his power; When he shall come to be glorified in his saints, and to be admired in all them that believe (because our

testimony among you was believed) in that day."

But a critic will say: "Ah, preacher, I cannot believe in such things. I cannot believe in hell, and I cannot believe in damnation, nor am I able to believe in the fires of punishment. I do not believe in the judgment and wrath of Almighty God." The only problem with such a view is this: the same revelation that speaks to us about hell is the same one that speaks to us about heaven. The same Bible that speaks of the love of God speaks of the wrath and judgment of Almighty God. If one is not true, then the other is not true. If there is not any fire and torment in hell, there are no golden streets and no pearly gates in glory. If there is not any Satan, there is not any Jesus Christ. If there is not anything to be saved from, there is no need for a man to preach salvation at all. It is because of the awful judgment of God, because of that everlasting torment, because of the reality of *Anathema,* that Jesus came into the world to be a Savior. There is a reason for his suffering and death. We are lost; we face the wrath and judgment of God. A man not in Christ is *Anathema.* Yet, immediately Paul says, "The grace of our Lord . . . be with you. My love be with you . . ." Wherever you have the true gospel preached, they will be right together, side by side, damnation and salvation.

The Lord Jesus who took little babes in his arms and blessed them is the same Lord Jesus who took a whip in his hand and drove out the money changers and denounced the hypocrisy of the Pharisees. The same story that tells us about Lazarus in the bosom of Abraham also tells us about the rich man who is tormented in hell. That description of torment is in the same book and in the same story, and it comes from the lips of the Lord Jesus. In 2 Corinthians 2:15-16 Paul says there is a savour of life unto life for those who believe, and a savour of death unto death for those who do not believe. When a man hears the gospel of the Son of God, he may repent and trust and be saved, but if that man rejects the gospel of Christ, he is lost and damned. The gospel of Christ is a two-edged sword, a two-fold message always and always.

The Compassionate Appeal of God

The critic continues: "Preacher, is that not a harsh thing for God to do, to tell us about those things of damnation and write them in the Book? And is that not an awful thing for a man to preach?" Yes, it is. It is a terrible thing. "Then why does God do it?" the critic asks. Simply because the gospel is the gospel. It is true—it faces reality. It is a merciful revelation from God to warn us about the reality of hell and how a man may escape with his life. The Bible is the most realistic Book in this earth, and it points out those terrible dangers and those horrible things that lie ahead for the soul without God and without Christ.

I say it is a merciful revelation because it is something God has given us out of his love for us. Whenever you come to a crossing on a railroad track, there may be an electric sign that will signal before an onrushing train, "Stop! Stop!" The sign is not there because the railroad company hates the people that cross over their property; it is there because the company knows the danger. When those great high speed freights come roaring by, the man about to cross the track will meet death if he does not stop. It is the same way with God. God says to us: "This road of unrighteousness leads to hell. Do not go that way!" The entreaties of God's people are like that: "This road of rejection leads to hell; turn and be saved." And the compassionate hearts of all who love and care for you cry out: "That road leads to hell. Do not go that way! Do not walk away without God! Do not spurn these pleadings of compassionate mercy and love! Hell and death are that way! Damnation is that way!" It is a twofold plea always of heaven and hell, if a man preaches the true gospel.

Love is that way, two-fold. For example, rebuke is the voice of love. Pleading against wrong and unrighteousness is the voice of somebody who cares. Are any of you men a father? When your son does wrong, what do you do with the boy? Do you not call the boy in and sit down by him and say: "Son, that road leads to damnation. Turn from that thing, son, do not go that way." Are any of you a mother? Do you not call your daughter in to sit down by your side and say: "Honey, that way is an awful way, and it leads down and down and down. Oh, precious child, do not go that way." Surely you do that because you love them. You love that boy, you love that girl, and you do not want to see them fall into hell.

Love pleads, cries, prays, and intercedes all day and all night and all the time in between. When your children are out in the night somewhere, if you are a good mother, the chances are you do not sleep until they return safely home. "Well," you say, "that is a silly thing to do." But that is a mother for you, that is love for you, and that is the way God is. "This road leads to hell, this is the way of damnation, this is *Anathema*," says the true God. Then in the next verse, "The grace of the Lord and my love be with you." That is the tenderness of God, that is the love of the Lord Jesus Christ.

Our Need of Compassionate Sympathy in the Church

Let me point out one other thing. What kind of folks were these that Paul is talking about? For one thing, they were as partisan and as divisive as they could be. One would stand up and say, "I am of Paul." Another would rise to avow, "I am of Apollos." Yet another would cry, "I am of Cephas" (1 Corinthians 1:12, 3:4). Not only that, but also there were some in that church who were unusually immoral. One fellow especially he describes as living in incest with his father's wife. Paul said that even the iniquitous Gentiles did not have a name for a fellow who would commit fornication with his own stepmother. Yet that evildoer was a member of the church (1 Corinthians 5:1). Not only that, but there were those who, when they came to the Lord's Supper, made gluttons of themselves at the Lord's table, and some of them got drunk. Paul was aghast (1 Corinthians 11:20). Furthermore, there were men in that church who stood up and said there is no such thing as a resurrection, and certainly no such thing as the resurrection of Jesus Christ (1 Corinthians 15:12). There were all kinds of moral and doctrinal problems in that church.

But what does Paul say about those people? Deploring their iniquity and pleading for their repentance, he writes: "The grace of our Lord Jesus Christ be with you. My love be with you all in Christ Jesus. Amen." That is the gospel. A fellow can be just as vile and iniquitous as he can be, but God puts his arms around him and the apostle puts his arms around him and loves him just the same. Here is a man who is a radical, and here is one who is divisive and partisan, and there is a man who deeply disappoints your soul. Should we call down the wrath of God on them? No, they must face the great and inevitable judgment of God upon the choices that they make, but we ought to cry over them and love them and plead with them just the same, just as God does. See how Paul responds, "My love be with you all." He put his arms about the whole church. Some of them were disappointing, some of them were denying the very gospel that he was preaching, some of them were living in open immorality, but Paul picked up his pen to write, "My love be with you all."

I would guess there is no finer picture of the gospel than a man with his arm around a fellow that needs Jesus, loving him into the Kingdom, praying over him for Jesus' sake. I do not care what the man is, or what he has done, the gospel is the Christian down on his knees with his arm around that fallen and needy brother, asking God to save him. That is the gospel. If a man is outside of Jesus, he is *Anathema. Maranatha*, the Lord comes. Are you ready? The most moving plea in the Scriptures is the plea of God to a fallen man that he turn and be saved (Ezekiel 18:23, 33:11).

4
The Waiting Christ at the Door of the Home

Behold, I stand at the door, and knock: if any man hear my voice, and open the door, I will come in to him, and will sup with him, and he with me (Revelation 3:20).

Revelation 3:20 falls in the context of the message to Laodicea, one of the seven Asian churches to whom our Lord addressed himself. In this message there is no word of commendation, but rather rebuke and condemnation. In this instance undoubtedly the worst has been saved for the last! To each of the other churches there is some good word. But there is nothing but blame for this last of the seven churches. Outside the home stands the living Christ, outside the door, outside the life of those who are domiciled within.

How can we estimate the number of homes in our land which fall into the Laodicean, lukewarm category—neither hot nor cold—neither hot and living nor cold and dead—just mediocre and in between. A great tragedy in Christendom today is the countless number of Christian homes in which families appear happy—the husband is not without headship but in between (unless his spouse really *knows* he is wrong, she honors his leadership) or the husband loves his wife as Christ loves the church except when she pushes him too far; the wife submits outwardly to her husband's headship but seethes with rebellion within; children honor their parents publicly to secure privileges but reject authority when their "personal rights" are violated or when the Holy Spirit "leads" them to do otherwise; parents demand obedience as long as it is convenient but cannot be bothered with responsibility for continual watching and training, or parents supervise homework and encourage Bible study and Scripture memorization when the child is old enough to do it himself, but these custodians of future generations cannot take time to teach and nurture the child from infancy in the riches of God's Word. Lukewarm families have the outer appearance of every success, but inside there is wretched poverty. Lukewarm families continue the masquerade of respectable harmony until their hypocrisy finally betrays them and they seek divorce.

The Traditional American Home Still Loved and Honored

American people in majority sentiment still honor the traditional home. The popular women's magazine *Better Homes and Gardens* sponsored a survey during the '70's which has revealed some interesting and thought-provoking data. Surprisingly enough, the magazine respondents overwhelmingly endorsed the traditional roles and values of the American family with such startling conclusions as these:

(1) Though most couples are not prepared for marriage when entering the blissful union, they are still happy with the system.

(2) People stay married because they love each other.

(3) Premarital and extra-marital sex do not contribute to a happy marriage.

(4) The traditional homemaking role for a woman is appropriate and little support was given to the idea that a woman needs a job or career to achieve fulfillment.

(5) A declining of the dominant role of the husband in the family is undesirable.[1]

Perhaps you are as amazed as I at such a forthright commendation and endorsement of the accustomed and biblical roles of husband and wife within the divinely-planned, one-flesh union, especially since these conclusions are coming from the public at random instead of the clergy or Christian laity. However, before we glibly pat ourselves on our backs to say what a good job we have done, let us look further at the survey.

Seventy-one per cent of the respondents (including people of all ages, at all educational levels, and of both sexes) indicated concern that family life in America is "in trouble." Out of ten choices for the single greatest threat to family life, the questionnaires were amazingly lucid in labeling with consensus the problems. They attributed this "trouble" first and foremost to materialism (37%) and permissive parents (29%) who are losing effective control over their children at a much earlier age than should be the case. Following these came drugs (18%), permissive attitudes about sex (14%), and divorce (12%). The popular catch-all answers to the world's problems which we so often lean upon and spend untold hours on, limitless funds, and boundless energy trying to solve—war, crime, pollution, overpopulation, Communism—were cited by only 3 to 5% of the respondents.

Is it possible that some of the American constituency is returning the horse to the front of the cart—could even a minority have the courage to go back to the beginning?

The Home in the Word and Plan of God

Before the "called-out assembly" *(ekklesia)* became the church, God instituted the home during the panorama of creation and placed this habitation in a garden paradise. Throughout the Bible we find continued inextricable concern and ineluctable direction given to this primary institution.

From the introduction of this clearly stated, divine design in Genesis we progress to the unveiling of the Decalogue in Exodus 20 in which every commandment touches upon some aspect of living within the family circle. Conspicuous within this concise presentation of God's law is the *only* commandment with promise—"Honor thy father and thy mother, that thy days may be long upon the land . . ."—and a pointed directive to the exclusiveness of the one-flesh relationship in the words, "Thou shalt not commit adultery," and the incisive warning that man must find satisfaction and contentment within the family circle, "Thou shalt not covet thy neighbor's house . . . wife . . . manservant."

In Leviticus with its precise delineation of divine law we find the penalty of death is due those who dare to prostitute the home.

In Numbers even the mundane task of numbering the people is to be done by families.

In Deuteronomy, the second giving of the Law, there is great emphasis on parental responsibility to instruct children as a parent sits, walks, lies down, rises up—which seems to be inclusive of just about every position known to me!

In Joshua the unquestioned headship of a patriarch who leads his family to stand on God's side can be observed.

In Judges we note Samson's lustful marriage to ungodliness, and the book of Ruth follows with its beautiful, poetic love story and marriage to godliness.

In the New Testament, Matthew, Mark, and Luke give account of the question raised by the Pharisees concerning divorce. Jesus points to the beginning one-flesh concept as his answer. In John's Gospel we find Jesus' first miracle at a wedding feast.

Acts presents contrasting couples—Ananias and Sapphira who agreed selfishly to withhold their possession from God; Aquila and Priscilla who in oneness selflessly gave themselves to the Lord in ministry.

The Corinthian epistles, Ephesians, Colossians, and 1 Peter—all are rich in teachings concerning inter-family relationships.

Alongside the scarlet thread of redemption from Genesis to Revelation we find our Father's teachings concerning the home—his picturesque illustration to us of the Father's love, the Son's sacrifice, and the Spirit's teaching.

Finally, we come to the consummative Apocalypse of the Apostle John for a special word concerning the last days:

"Behold, I stand at the door, and knock; if any man hear my voice, and open the door, I will come in to him, and will sup with him, and he with me." (Revelation 3:20).

The Savior's Knocking at the Door

How typical of our Savior's compassionate outpouring is the inclusion of this hopeful word for as seemingly a hopeless situation as the one at Laodicea! He never forgets us or lets us down. Corrie ten Boom shared in our beloved church an experience from her bleak and lengthy confinement in the Ravensbruck concentration camp. There came some days of intolerable cruelty as one of the ruthless guards insisted upon venting his barbarous hostility upon selected prisoners during the daily roll call. Even for those watching empathetically, the vicarious pain of such inhumanity was almost unbearable. However, the very first morning this wretchedness began, Miss ten Boom noticed a skylark in the heavens chirping in melodious tones a soothing melody of joy. The other prisoners caught the sweet strains. Day after day just at the moment of horror, this small creature appeared with its song of cheer. Even thus do we find these words of our Lord to the nauseous, lukewarm Laodiceans. The warm invitation of a loving Savior is a blessed hope, even for the most hopeless.

Truly, this incisive verse of Revelation 3:20 from the pen of the beloved apostle John speaks directly to the homes of America. The word *krouō,* meaning "knock," is in the present tense and consequently may well be paraphrased: "I continue knocking day in and day out." On the other hand, the very *estēka,* meaning "stand," is in the perfect tense and can thus be paraphrased: "I have stood, I will stand, I will keep on and on standing." From the beginning the Creator has shown his interest and concern for his first institution. This glorious design came from the Edenic paradise when God created man with an inherent need and desire for a perfect counterpart, which the gracious Father then supplied to Adam. These two—man and woman—made in His image, were the first pages of God's theological textbook—his revealing of himself in and to mankind.

In the relationship of husband and wife we see one of the best explanations of the relationships within the Godhead. Here are two perfect creations equal in essence—both created in the image of God and thus equal before him—both coming to God through the mediator Jesus Christ (Galatians 3:28). However, there is not this equality or "sameness" in responsibility and function. Just as we see the Son subordinate and submit himself to the will of the Father in his earthly mission, accordingly God's assignment in the home is for the man to exercise loving headship and the woman to submit in obedient example. From the analogy of Father and Son we can move to the picture of Christ and his church. The church was made perfect by atonement through his cleansing blood, becoming joint-heirs with Jesus and consequently fellow-children by divinely irrevocable adoption; yet Jesus Christ still retains headship over his church and demands obedient living in submission to his lordship from all disciples.

Only By Invitation Does Christ Come In

Coming back to the invitation given to the Laodicean church, one can project a very possible literal interpretation—Jesus Christ has, is, and will stand at the doors of homes throughout the world knocking continually until the time of his return. That same love which prompted him to leave the riches of heaven at his incarnation impels him to entreat and plead even yet in his aggressive seeking after those for whom he died. Yet, he created us with a door—individual freedom of choice to be exercised through intellectual and emotional consideration. He will neither violate our moral freedom nor crush our volitional choice. God had a design; he instituted that perfect plan in Eden; he gave direct commandment and teaching for making the plan work; he declared and proved his loving concern to encourage us in our weakness; but he will not force open the door. Jesus will enter our homes only by invitation, preceded by our unlocking the doors and opening them in genuine hospitality to his divine presence. Then he not only enters, but also enjoys fellowship with us. *Deipnesō* is the future tense. It is not like the standing which began in the past and continued on or the knocking which goes on day after day, but the eating or dining within the home is a state of continuing fellowship to come in the future as a result of positive action to the entreaty of our living Lord.

Christ in the home makes all things new, fresh, and heavenly, just as his presence adds the celestial benediction to our mansion in the heavenly home, the New Jerusalem. As the glory of God is seen in our home in the sky, so is the glory of God seen in the Christian home in the earth. Paul has reminded us that we are "living letters known and read of all men" (2 Corinthians 3:2). Nowhere in God's creation is there a more precise and vivid theological textbook than the Christian home. The family unit bearing the name of our Lord gives a "word about God" (the word "theology" means literally this) with every day that goes by. The Christian home is a divine benediction to every passing day.

The Christian Home According to the Word of God

In Ephesians 5:22—6:4 the Apostle Paul by divine inspiration has written for us the spirit and attitude of those who make up the Christian home. His words are full of deepest love and meaning. He says that husbands are to love their wives as Christ loved the church. This love is a sacrificial love, for Jesus loved enough to die for his church. His love was a servant love, for he ministered to his disciples and followers, even to the point of complete humiliation in washing the dusty, travel-weary feet of the apostles who shunned such a lowly task. His love continues to be everlastingly with us, for even as we fail him, disappoint him, hurt him, humiliate him, still he loves us—praise his holy name!

Husbands, then, must be willing to sacrifice their time to minister to their precious wives—talk to them, listen to them, take them to a concert even when it would be more interesting to the man to see the football game on television; give up the golf clubs to pay for that expensive dress she has been admiring in the department store window. Husbands must be willing to do the menial tasks of diapering the baby while the wife enjoys a much needed nap, helping with the dishes on nights when she is especially tired, preparing her food when she is sick—serving her when she has not the strength to serve herself and the family. Husbands must love on and on unto the ages of the ages—when she is cross and curt; when she nags and annoys; when she fails to do what she promised; when she fumbles the ball on an important plan; when she is selfish and forgetful, when she is rebellious. Only when we have loved as Christ loved can husbands exercise the headship God assigned. This is the divine word of the Bible.

Wives, submit yourselves unto your own husbands, as unto the Lord. The word for submit is *hupotassō,* meaning "to line up under" or "to come under the protection of." Submission is a total commitment; it is not only an obedient act, but also a deferential attitude prompted by the "meek and quiet spirit," about which Peter wrote. Your husband's leadership is not only a law controlling your actions but also an ordinance honored in your heart. The key unlocking this principle is the spiritual understanding that your submission is "as unto the Lord." The headship of your husband is planned not only to protect you, but also to free you for creativity within your own sphere of responsibility. What husband does not prize the intuitive discernment of a submissive wife?

Parents (not Sunday School teachers, Vacation Bible School leaders, etc.)—you teach your children God's law and train and nurture them in the Word. What a difference there would be in the coming generations if from childhood they were taught by parents and grandparents the precious Word of God through the family altar and individual instruction to supplement the Christian education of the church.

Children, obey your parents in the Lord. When a child bends his will to a parent in complete obedience, how great is his lesson on how to relate to his heavenly Father! To obey the father whom he can see, whose love he can experience in many tangible ways, whose presence is visible to see and touch—this is a natural prelude to the childlike response he must have toward the perfect heavenly Father who also demands perfect obedience, unfolds measureless love, and reveals himself to those who seek his face.

How vital—how indispensable is the Christian home UNTIL JESUS COMES BACK! It is Jesus himself who knocks at the doors of our homes.

---

1. A Report on the American Family from the Editors of *Better Homes and Gardens*, Meredith Corp., 1972, pp. 3, 4, 6.

5
The Golden Tomorrow

Not as though I had already attained, either were already perfect: but I follow after, if that I may apprehend that for which also I am apprehended of Christ Jesus.
Brethren, I count not myself to have apprehended: but this one thing I do, forgetting those things which are behind, and reaching forth unto those things which are before,
I press toward the mark for the prize of the high calling of God in Christ Jesus. . . .
For our conversation is in heaven; from whence also we look for the Saviour, the Lord Jesus Christ: Who shall change our vile body, that it may be fashioned like unto his glorious body, according to the working whereby he is able even to subdue all things unto himself (Philippians 3:12-14, 20-21).

To read the third chapter of Philippians is to be astonished at the two things Paul places almost in the same breath. He first speaks of his taking hold of the thing for which God took hold of him. "Not as though I had already attained it or am already perfected, but I follow after," he says, "if that I may *katalambano*, if I may get hold of, if I may seize, that for which God got hold of me."

The whole passage is taken from the imagery of Greek public games, from the Olympics. While watching those games, Paul saw, by God's inspiration, how he could use the words and the language of the contest to express his Christian experience. For example, when he says, "that I may *katalambano*" he chose the word the Greeks used for the seizing, the taking, the winning of the prize. He continues: "Brethren, I count not myself to have seized it yet; I have not won it yet. But this one thing I do, I *dioko*, I press, I reach, I stretch toward the mark for the prize of the high calling of God in Christ Jesus."

Then Paul speaks of the other side of that golden triumph: "For our conversation, our *politeuma*, is in heaven." *Polis* is the Greek word for "city," and *polites* refers to a "citizen." Thus, *politeuma*, the word Paul uses here, indicates the condition or life of a citizen and is better translated "citizenship." "For our citizenship is in heaven, from whence also we look for the Saviour, the Lord Jesus Christ, who, when he comes, is able even to subdue all things unto himself." The golden tomorrow. Here we have our assignment and our work; we are to be reaching forth to get hold of the thing for which God got hold of us, to be doing the things to which Christ has called us. We stretch, we run, we reach forth, yet at the same time we are watching and waiting for and believing in the personal, visible, triumphant return of our Lord from heaven. There is a deeply significant meaning for us in the juxtaposition of those two thoughts: to work, to be faithful, to strive, and at the same time to wait and believe, to pray and watch for the return of our Christ from glory.

I think of the old farmer who was out in the field plowing. A neighbor came by to visit with him, evidently having attended a service on the second coming of the Lord at church, for he asked his friend, "If you knew that the Lord would come back in the next thirty minutes, what would you do?" The godly farmer replied, "I would plow this furrow to the end of the row." That is right! We are to be working, striving, serving, and at the same time, watching, waiting, and praying, for that golden tomorrow.

God's Purpose for Us

First, let us think of the striving, of the getting hold, of the doing of that for which Christ has called us. In Philadelphia, in Independence Hall, I looked at the chair in which George Washington sat as he presided over the Constitutional Convention. On the back of that chair is a sunburst—the sun at the horizon with the rays of light pouring out from it. When the convention had written the greatest political document in human history, the Constitution of the United States of America, aged Ben Franklin stood up and said, "During these days and days I have been looking at that sunburst, and I have been wondering whether it was a sunset or a sunrise." Then the great statesman added, "After seeing what has been done in the adoption of this instrument, the Constitution of the United States of America, I have come to see that it is a sunrise." How little did the aged Franklin realize that America would grow in power and in strength far beyond any man's wildest imagination back there in the 1700's when that document was framed.

So it is, I think, for the work of the people in our dear church in Dallas, and I pray that the same might be true for every pastor or deacon anywhere in the world who reads these words. There is a sunrise, a golden tomorrow to seek after, if we will be faithful in doing the thing for which God has chosen us. May I mention a few of those golden tomorrows out of my own experience.

One of the dreams of my life in the more than thirty years of this pastorate has been to have a school here, using these vast facilities in the daytime. I wanted a school where the children could be taught, not just for a fifty-minute period on a Sunday morning, but for hours every day. Oh, that would be an incomparable opportunity if it could be seized!

As we began the school in the fall of 1972, Principal Mel Carter asked, "Pastor, would you speak to our first chapel service?" I went to Embree Hall and saw the children come in there with their Christian principal and their dedicated Christian teachers. First of all, they quoted for me my favorite Bible verse, Isaiah 40:8. "The grass withereth, the flower fadeth, but the word of our God shall stand forever." Then they sang songs of heaven. As I sat there and looked at the teachers and looked at the children and thought of the years of the dream and the vision, I brushed the tears from my eyes. And that was just the beginning. By the spring of 1975 our enrollment had increased almost fourfold. God sent those youngsters to receive their elementary and high school education in a distinctively Christian atmosphere. This is just the start and the earnest of a more glorious day that is yet to come.

Another golden tomorrow comes to my mind. It had for years been my thought to have a Bible Institute here in our church and to invite pastors and laymen and laywomen and church leaders and staff members who do not attend seminaries to come and to share the riches of God's Word together. I had not thought, however, to begin it so soon, yet we started it in September of 1970. Some of the people around me said, "Pastor, why not just start?" "Well," I said, "we do not have anything ready; we have not prepared." "Well, just begin," they argued. So we did. With volunteer help, with our own staff employed in other areas in the church, we just began our Bible Institute that September.

From the beginning, from the first day, the infinite pleasure and celestial benedictory blessing of God has been upon it. Our trustees and board members prayed that God would lead us to that one man in all the earth that the Lord had chosen to head this work. To my own gladness beyond any way for me to describe it, the Lord led us and him so that one of the most gifted and experienced theologians in our generation, Dr. H. Leo Eddleman, came to help us build that glorious institution. Then in February of 1975, God brought us Dr. Paige Patterson, an outstanding young theologian in our Baptist world, to take up the reigns and lead our institute as its new president. During the spring semester of 1975 we had already reached an excellent day enrollment, and our total enrollment counting those in our night school program was well over 1,000. Oh, what is bound up in the possibilities of that work! Teaching preachers and staff members, Sunday School leaders, deacons, church leaders, teaching them the Word of the Lord! In a thousand ways is that door opened to us by the Spirit of God and it portends another golden tomorrow.

Then I think of our own teaching ministries here in the church, our Sunday School, our Training Union, our missionary organizations, our music program, our recreational program, and the vast outreach of our mission work both in the city and beyond. It is unbelievably wonderful just to look upon it. For example, during 1973-74 our regular Sunday School organizations averaged 5,886 individuals engaged in Bible study every Sunday from October to March. For those same Sundays (October through March) in 1974-75 God increased that weekly average attendance to 6,635. It astonishes me to think of what lies ahead in the expanding of that teaching ministry. The soon-coming of Christ does not send us to our rocking chair to relax and wait! The nearness of the final consummation does not send us to the hills wearing "ascension robes"! Believing that Jesus is coming soon sends us back into the world to "reach for the mark for the prize of our high calling in Christ Jesus," to strive to accomplish that which God has set before us.

We have just completed a $3,300,000 Christian Education Building, and so dynamic and viable and quickened is the onrush and the outreach of this church that before that building was finished, we had more than enough people to fill it to overflowing. We will need another one. During this year our people will easily give over $5,000,000 to the work of Christ in the earth. What a vast sum for our church to give year by year! It is astonishing, it is overwhelming what is happening in this church. I just thank God that I was around when the Lord chose to do it. But I can also see that if we are to do this thing for which God got hold of us to do, if we are to seize that for which also we are seized by the Lord Jesus, if we are to reach out and possess the thing God has called us to possess, it will involve vast consecration on our part. As the apostle says here, "Brethren, I do not have it yet, I have not yet arrived, but this one thing I do, I *diokō,* I press, I strive toward the prize for the high calling of God in Christ Jesus."

I need not point out to you, my fellow soldiers in Christ, that whatever God may have set before us, whether large or small, none of us can do these things indifferently, or even optionally; it demands of us a dynamic, fundamental commitment to the ministry Christ has given us. I must support it, largely, greatly, deeply, Sunday by Sunday, month by month, year after year. It commands from us our utmost, our best, if there is to be a golden tomorrow.

God's Promise to Us

We must be working, striving, reaching out, yet at the same time watching, waiting, working, praying because our *politeuma* (our citizenship) is in heaven, "from whence also we look for the Saviour, the Lord Jesus Christ." This is also what Paul calls our blessed hope. We are watching, waiting, and working until the ultimate day shall finally come, and He shall subdue all things unto Himself.

The coming of our Lord is always imminent, always at hand, yet we are to work and to serve in every generation however long he may tarry. In Revelation 22:20, we read: "He which testifieth these things saith, Surely, I come quickly." That is a clear testimony to the imminency of the return of our Lord and to the triumph that he bears with him in his gracious and nail-pierced hands. But also we read in Revelation 2:26: "And he that overcometh, and keepeth my works unto the end, to him will I give power over the nations." This is no less a clear testimony to the work we are to do until Jesus comes.

On Mt. Zion in Jerusalem is the traditional tomb of King David. Also on Mt. Zion in Jerusalem is the traditional site of the Upper Room where the Holy Spirit came down on the

120 disciples. On Mt. Zion there is yet another shrine to visit, namely, a display of the horrors that the Jewish people suffered in the Nazi and Communist persecutions. From exhibit to exhibit you can find the Torah, the books of the Mosaic Law, bathed in human blood, as the officiating rabbis were slain while presiding over their synagogue services. There are the vestments, stained in Jewish blood, that were ripped to shreds as the bayonets cut the rabbis to pieces. Another of the exhibits is a great circle containing the ashes of many of those who were forced into the gas chambers, or shot down before the firing squads. In the center is a glass case full of soap, made of human flesh, human fat; soap made out of Jewish flesh. By the side of that glass case on a plaque formed in a triangle shape pointing upward toward heaven, there is in Hebrew the song that the Jewish people sang as they faced martyrdom, faced the gas chamber, faced the firing squad, faced the bullet and the bayonet. There is the song that they sang written in large Hebrew letters, and a literal translation of that song, by the side of the soap, is this:

> "Of all the truth, this is the truth that we most believe: Messiah is coming soon. Despite the fact He has not come today, despite any other facts in life, this is the truth that we believe: Messiah is coming soon."

Facing martyrdom and death, they sang that song. That is what Paul is speaking of: striving, reaching, apprehending God's choice and will for us; yet at the same time, strengthened and comforted in the knowledge that our Messiah, Christ, is coming soon.

As I think of those Jewish people, millions of them martyred, persecuted, slain; and others still in certain areas of the earth hated and slaughtered; and as I think of their devotion to the faith of Moses and the old covenant, O God, what of us, what of me?

Am I soldier of the cross,
A follower of the Lamb,
And shall I fear to own His cause
Or blush to speak His name?

Must I be carried to the skies
On flow'ry beds of ease,
While others fought to win the prize
And sailed thro' bloody seas?

Are there no foes for me to face?
Must I not stem the flood?
Is this vile world a friend to grace,
To help me on to God?

Sure I must fight if I would reign;
Increase my courage, Lord;
I'll bear the toil, endure the pain,
Supported by Thy word.

                                        ISAAC WATTS

Ah, what blessedness and fullness and glory God has promised to us who love him, who work, who watch, who wait, who believe, who trust, and who walk into the future in the confidence and assurance that victory in Christ shall assuredly be placed in our hands. Be faithful, Christian soldier; Christ is coming soon! Maranatha!